Welcome to the Kingdom

How to Live a 21st Century Kingdom Life

Dana Carson, D.Min., Ph.D.

WESTBOW
PRESS®
A DIVISION OF THOMAS NELSON
& ZONDERVAN

Scripture taken from the New King James Version®. Copyright © 1982 by Thomas Nelson. Used by permission. All rights reserved.

This book is a work of non-fiction. Unless otherwise noted, the author and the publisher make no explicit guarantees as to the accuracy of the information contained in this book and in some cases, names of people and places have been altered to protect their privacy.

WestBow Press books may be ordered through booksellers or by contacting:

WestBow Press
A Division of Thomas Nelson & Zondervan
1663 Liberty Drive
Bloomington, IN 47403
www.westbowpress.com
1 (866) 928-1240

Because of the dynamic nature of the Internet, any web addresses or links contained in this book may have changed since publication and may no longer be valid. The views expressed in this work are solely those of the author and do not necessarily reflect the views of the publisher, and the publisher hereby disclaims any responsibility for them.

Any people depicted in stock imagery provided by Thinkstock are models, and such images are being used for illustrative purposes only. Certain stock imagery © Thinkstock.

ISBN: 978-1-9736-0193-7 (sc)
ISBN: 978-1-9736-0192-0 (e)

Library of Congress Control Number: 2017914608

Print information available on the last page.

WestBow Press rev. date: 01/15/2018

Introduction

W E ARE LIVING IN a very pivotal time in history. Life and culture as we knew them have passed away, and we are experiencing the dawning of a new day—the day of church past. This may sound like the ghost from the Charles Dickins classic, *A Christmas Carol,* but we are really living in a time when Christianized America no longer finds confidence and comfort in the scriptures or the church. Our young people are exiting the church in great numbers, the church attrition rate is soaring, and pulpit abandonment is common. The church has to hear the lyrics of famous R&B singer Marvin Gaye in their heads: "What's going on, I said, what's going on?"

The church was once the solid foundation that America rested upon, to such an extent that religious documents such as baptism certificates were considered legal documents. If you were not affiliated with a church, you were stigmatized by everyone. Every good American had a church and a pastor, who was responsible for teaching him or her wholesome Bible principles that would increase the probability of success in life. The church was both significant and prominent in the minds of most Americans. However, it has become a moral nuisance to this immoral, contemporary society and has lost its social luster. The church is currently undergoing social rejection by Western society and is having a very uncomfortable time handling this rejection. The church has become a social institution that is based upon racism, classism, sexism, denominationalism, and egotism and has lost its direction and identity. The church was created to be an instrument and a guiding light into kingdom living but has instead become a vassal for Westernized European culture. The church was created to usher people into the kingdom and serve as an embassy of God's kingdom on Earth.

This book is designed to help provide some insight and assistance to 21st century believers who desire to live wholly and completely for Christ the King. The challenge of the 21st century church is submission to the crown of Christ and not getting totally intoxicated by the cross of Christ. The cross was designed to present us to the crown of Christ so that we may come to know Christ not simply as the Lamb that was slain but also the Lion that rules and reigns. Our new life in Christ is a new life in the kingdom of God. Christ was incarnate for redemption and revelation; however, He came to save and to instruct. Christ spent His entire life teaching about the kingdom of God, but unfortunately, today we only know about the church. Living in the kingdom and attending church are not synonymous. Church membership can be defined, in the most purist traditional sense, as being committed to the local church through tithes and offerings, attendance, and participation in church ministries. While the traditional definitions and expectations of church members are clearly biblical responsibilities of every believer, these do not define life in the kingdom. Living in the kingdom is not a static experience but rather a dynamic, interactive lifestyle that I hope to make clear in the pages of this book. Now let's explore what it means to enter the kingdom.

Chapter One
The Church and the Kingdom

B ECOMING A PART OF the kingdom is essential to a walk and a relationship with God. However, Christ taught us that His kingdom is not of this world; therefore, when we enter the kingdom, we enter into a spiritual sphere of existence that is full of spiritual realities that are much different than living as a natural citizen. The ministry and total focus of Christ was the message of the kingdom, and He provided access to the kingdom through His life and death.

Christ taught us everything we need to know in this life about the kingdom, and when we grasp its value, we will press into the kingdom passionately. Unfortunately, one of the biggest hindrances to entering into the kingdom today is joining the church. While the church is a critical organism in the kingdom, it was never intended to be the ultimate in the kingdom. The church was designed to merely be the path to the kingdom. The concept of the church was introduced to us by the Messiah Himself. Christ designed her as His property and placed her on Earth to serve as the embassy of His kingdom. The concept of the church is a New Testament creation; there was no church proper in the Old Testament, although we can discuss the structure of Israel in light of the church concept, but the church is literally a New Testament phenomenon. Jesus built the church upon the revelation that He is the Son of God, which was not known in the Old Testament.

He said to them, "But who do you say that I am?" Simon Peter answered and said, "You are the Christ, the Son of the living God." Jesus answered and said to him, "Blessed are you, Simon Bar-Jonah, for flesh and blood has not revealed this to you, but My Father who is in heaven. And I also say to you that you are Peter, and on this rock I will build My church, and the gates of Hades shall not prevail against it. And I will give you the keys of the kingdom of heaven, and whatever you bind on earth will be bound in heaven, and whatever you loose on earth will be loosed in heaven."[1]

Because most people do not know what the church is or its primary function, they are confused about what the kingdom is and the difference between the kingdom and the church. As a result of this ignorance, the church has become something vastly different from what God intended it to be; thus, education about the church and the kingdom is necessary.

Two of the most controversial and misunderstood theological concepts in the Bible are the kingdom of God and the church. The kingdom of God is not the church, and the church is not the kingdom of God. Unfortunately, because we do not know how to interpret the church in light of the kingdom of God, the church has developed into a sociological phenomenon that reflects the culture of our society and the wishes of the people rather than the intentions for which God created it: an institution that is inspired by and reflective of the kingdom of God.

The Kingdom vs. the Church

Let's examine some of the differences between the kingdom and the church by first looking at the kingdom. When we discuss the topic of the kingdom of God, we are speaking of the rule of God, the reign of God, and the realm of God. When men and women enter the

---

[1] Matthew 16:15–19 (NKJV).

kingdom, they submit their hearts to the authority of God, and His rule and reign bring them to a place of total submission. When God established a covenant with man, He did so as a kingdom covenant. The terms of this covenant were to be lived out in the framework of the kingdom with God as the king. When God delivered Israel from Egyptian bondage and then through the Reed or Red Sea, Moses and the children of Israel cried aloud, "Our God reigns!" Reigning is what a king does; thus, Israel recognized that their emancipation was attributed to God the King, who reigns over Pharaoh and all the kings of the earth (Exodus 15:18).

When we discuss the kingdom proper and the church proper, it should be noted that any reference to the church in the Old Testament is just a type and shadow analogy; as stated earlier, the church is a New Testament creation. Scholars sometimes make reference to Israel as a church as a teaching tool or a model of organization that demonstrates how Israel functioned as an organized people. However, I want to make sure that it is clear that the church is a New Testament phenomenon only. Israel functioned as a spiritual and political kingdom that was subject to Yahweh through His civil, religious, and moral laws. So, Dr. Carson, what's the point here? The point is that the kingdom is clearly not the church and the church is not the kingdom (Matthew 16:19).

John Fullenbach's book, *The Kingdom of God*, states that the kingdom is more comprehensive than the term "church." Being in the church is not synonymous with being in the kingdom, because the kingdom is much broader and more comprehensive than the church. In fact, the kingdom is what created the church.

The discussion of the kingdom is beyond information; it is an experience. As we continue to discuss becoming a kingdom citizen and living in the kingdom, it means allowing God to rule and reign in your life as King on both a daily and theoretical basis. If God is not establishing your direction and guiding your decisions based on His will, then you cannot be seeking first the kingdom of God (Matthew 6:33). If you are not totally submitting yourself to God through His Word, your life is not totally submitted to Him—even if you go to church week in and week out.

The concept of the kingdom is much vaster than that of the church. In fact, the church was born out of the kingdom; the kingdom was not born out of the church. The church was created by the kingdom, not vice versa. When it comes to the church and the kingdom, we must be mindful of the fact that the kingdom is an eternal institution and not time based. The kingdom can exist without the church, but the church cannot exist without the kingdom. The church age is terminal, which means it will end in the event commonly referred to as "the rapture" of the church. The church is the local agency of the kingdom built on the death, burial, and resurrection of Christ and is commissioned to usher people into the kingdom until the church age ends. After the church is withdrawn from the earth, she will no longer serve a purpose since she was designed to lead people to Christ and His kingdom: "And I will give you the keys of the kingdom...."[2]

St. Augustine held the position that there was both a visible and an invisible church. The visible church is comprised of the churches that we see here on Earth—the tangible, concrete church. The invisible church is comprised of the body of believers that we cannot see—those who have been born again and placed into God's church since the church was born. According to St. Augustine, it is possible to be a part of the visible church without being a part of the invisible church, and this happens far too often. People join the visible church without being born again into the invisible church. Thus, the visible church is comprised of both believers and unbelievers. However, the invisible church is comprised only of believers.

---

[2] Matthew 16:19 (NKJV).

The Kingdom Defined

The kingdom of God can be defined as "God's rule and reign in the hearts of men who submit themselves to the sovereign will and plan of God for their lives as kingdom citizens." Kingdom citizens are the subjects of God's kingdom who exist in the realm of God and submit to the rule of God as they honor the reign of God. Kingdom citizens are not simply people who are dedicated to a church; they are those who have surrendered their plans for their lives to what God has planned for them. Kingdom citizens have prioritized the King's will for their lives over and above their own.

The kingdom of God is comprised of people who have submitted their lives to the plan of God, allowing His plan to overtake any plans they might have had for their own lives. God has a plan for your life; He created you with a purpose in mind that will never change regardless of where you go or what you do. When you submit yourself to what God created you for and to the parameters that He has established for your life, only then can you live in the kingdom as one of His citizens.

The Church vs. the Kingdom

George Ladd, who is a highly recognized author and New Testament theologian, writes in his work entitled *The Gospel of the Kingdom* a very thought-provoking discourse on Matthew 16:17–19.

- The church is not the kingdom.
- The kingdom created the church.
- The church bears witness to the kingdom.
- The church is the instrument of the kingdom.
- The church is the custodian of the kingdom.

The church is different from the kingdom in that the King created the church and uses it to accomplish His purpose here on Earth.

The church is not the kingdom of God. Those who are unlearned in the things of the kingdom may promote that the church is "just another way" of saying the kingdom, but they refer to two very distinct, different things. The church and the kingdom are not synonymous.

The kingdom created the church. The church did not create the kingdom. Since the kingdom created the church, the church has a responsibility to serve the kingdom by being a witness and serving as an instrument and a custodian.

The church bears witness to the kingdom. It is the role of the church to bear witness to the kingdom. In other words, the church testifies to people that the kingdom exists. It is the church's duty to inform people about kingdom principles, practices, and culture. However, even though the church has existed for two thousand years, at some point, she lost sight of her role and responsibility to witness to the reality of the kingdom. As a result of not focusing on this responsibility, the church began to focus on and testify about itself. The result of the church's inadequate job of communicating the culture and the message of the kingdom is that people are now ignorant as it relates to the kingdom. They know very little about the kingdom and a great deal about the church.

The church is the instrument of the kingdom. An instrument is something that you use to accomplish a purpose or task; thus, the kingdom uses the church to accomplish the goals of evangelism and kingdom expansion. The church is what the eternal kingdom of God uses to do its business here on Earth. The church is an instrument or a means, not an end. Thus, the church is not the destination but simply a means by which people can enter the kingdom.

The church is the custodian of the kingdom. A custodian is someone who is responsible for taking care of a particular place, and he or she always has the keys! If you need to get into a locked room in the facility, you call the custodian, right? Well, in essence, the church is the "janitor" of the kingdom of God. Because the church holds the keys to the kingdom, it is responsible for allowing people access into the kingdom of God. The analogy of the church being the janitor is not meant to be a statement of dishonor or a devaluing of the church but simply to suggest that it serves the kingdom and makes entrance into it possible through the keys to the kingdom.

Dr. Brad Young, in his book, *Jesus, the Jewish Theologian*, states, "Jesus viewed the kingdom of heaven as an active force in the world that was energized by God's power. The gospels are inundated with the message of the kingdom; however, the church is largely ignorant concerning Christ and the kingdom."[3] If you are a kingdom citizen, you understand that you are a compelling, dynamic witness who is energized by the very power of the kingdom of God to be a change agent in the lives of others, just like they did in the gospels and the New Testament church. Dr. Young sees the presence of the kingdom of God as an active force in the world that is energized by God and makes people radically active in witnessing about the kingdom and the things of God. When you are in the kingdom of God, you are not shy; you can't stop talking about the kingdom! The New Testament church was focused on the kingdom message and was known as "those who turned the world upside down" (Acts 17:6). The early church was a radical church.

When you are a citizen of the kingdom of God, you do not simply wait for God to come back to get you while you sit idly by watching what is going on around you; instead, you recognize that you are a change agent who is proactive and aggressive! You are empowered by a dynamic and energetic force to transform the lives of the people of God in Jerusalem, Judea, Samaria, and the uttermost parts of the earth with the message of the kingdom. Kingdom scholar Craig Van Gelder states, "Coming to clarity on the meaning of the kingdom of God is foundational to understanding the mission of

---

[3] Brad H. Young, Jesus the Jewish Theologian (Grand Rapids: Baker Academic, 1995).

God in the world."[4] It is impossible to carry out God's mission on Earth without understanding the kingdom, because the kingdom dictates what we are here to accomplish on Earth.

As a lawyer, if you are not crystal clear about the practice of law, you will not be able to understand your purpose in the courtroom when you stand with your client. You won't know what you're doing if you do not know what you're trying to accomplish and why you're trying to accomplish it. You're surely going to be off in what you're doing! In the same fashion, Van Gelder says that if you do not understand the kingdom of God with clarity, there is no way that you can properly execute the mission of the church. Thus, if you are ignorant of the kingdom of God, it is very safe to assume that your church is "off" with regard to accomplishing its mission. Why? Because it is the kingdom of God that gives definition to the church's function!

The kingdom of God was the primary emphasis of the gospels, the book of Acts, and the general and pastoral Pauline epistles—not the church. Jesus preached the kingdom of God, not the church. The reason we preach and teach heavily concerning the kingdom is because it is what Jesus Himself preached. Jesus did not teach about the church. In fact, He only talks about the church in Matthew 16 and Matthew 18. No other time in the gospels do we see Jesus talking about the church. As His church, we want to preach and teach what Jesus preached and taught, and the gospels are inundated with the focus on the kingdom of God. None of the rest of the gospels (Mark, Luke, and John) discuss the topic of the church; however, we know that it was and is a very important aspect of the kingdom. From the synoptic gospels (Matthew, Mark, and Luke) to the Johannine gospel, you will hear the kingdom of God theme over and over again. The kingdom is obviously and undeniably the most prevalent theme of the gospels. On the

---

[4] Craig Van Gelder, The Essence of the Church: A Community Created by the Spirit (Grand Rapids: BakerBooks, 2000).

contrary, we do not hear the theme of the church in the gospels (except Matthew 16 and 18). This does not mean that the church is not important; however, it does mean that the church is subject to the kingdom of God. Jesus' concern was that we understand the kingdom of God, not simply the church.

The book of Acts begins and ends with a focus on the kingdom of God. At the beginning of Acts, the disciples met with Jesus after His resurrection, and they asked Him about the kingdom of God (Acts 1:6). Note that this is the disciples' final conversation with Christ, and they are preoccupied with one thing: the kingdom (not the church!). The kingdom must have been important! The disciples wanted to know if Jesus was about to return the kingdom to Jewish control—something the Jews had been waiting on for many years. Jesus was about to give birth to the church through the Holy Spirit, but they did not ask Him about this; their sole concern was the kingdom. Then, at the end of Acts, the very last two verses of the book (28:30–31) tell us Paul taught on the kingdom in a rented house. This is how consumed the early church was with the kingdom of God.

As mentioned earlier, the church is the embassy of the kingdom, which is why Paul refers to himself and the other apostles as ambassadors of the kingdom (2 Corinthians 5:20). What is an ambassador? An ambassador is an official representative at the highest level who represents a foreign country in a sovereign state. An ambassador is responsible for spreading the principles of his or her own country in that country. An ambassador is the head of the embassy, and the embassy, which is the church, represents the interests of the kingdom of God and kingdom citizens.

Every kingdom has to have citizens, or people who are officially recognized as being a part of the kingdom, with all of the corresponding rights and responsibilities of citizenship. We are citizens of two kingdoms—two worlds—but our primary citizenship is in heaven. You and I are foreigners or sojourners while we are here on Earth; however, it is safe and politically acceptable for us to be here because our king has influence in this territory. In fact, our king has an embassy here. That embassy is called the "church." World travelers know that the very first place you should go when you arrive in a foreign country (if you are not too overly optimistic) is to the embassy. The embassy is your home nation's representation in that foreign country. Upon arrival, you should immediately go to the embassy to check in and let your country's representatives know that you are there. This is necessary because if a crisis develops, the embassy will then know exactly where you are staying and how to reach you. If necessary, they will get you out of that country to protect your safety. The embassy is responsible for you while you are there on foreign soil because you are a citizen of their country. Thank God that you are a citizen of the kingdom of God, because when chaos and destruction occur in the end, the King Himself will come to get His people and take them to safety. Citizenship in the kingdom does matter! When the rapture of the church occurs, only kingdom citizens will be rescued. However, you must have your kingdom passport and show proof of citizenship to be allowed in!

The church is a very important aspect of the kingdom, although they are not one and the same, since those who enter the kingdom must do so through the ministry of the church. However, we must be concerned about the fact that in our contemporary church world, we discuss everything through the lens of the church, not through the lens of the kingdom. Because of the church's deficiency of discussions concerning the kingdom, it has left room for many false teachers and cults to invade the world of the Bible and give the church a non-kingdom message and agenda. This has caused many to abandon the church.

We know that the church was a prophetic entity that was yet to come at Pentecost; thus, in the book of Acts, we hear a great deal about the church and its growth and expansion as a kingdom embassy spreading the good news of the kingdom around the world. The book of Acts records that after Peter's message on Pentecost, thousands of souls were added to the church. Peter's message of Christ being Lord and Savior was the foundation that the church was built upon. Peter preached the revelation that was given him in Matthew 16: Christ the Son of the Living God and the outpouring of the Holy Spirit according to the prophesies of Joel. People were saved and entered the kingdom and then placed in the church to serve. As kingdom citizens, we are saved; we enter the kingdom of God through being born again, and then we are made to sit together in Christ Jesus in heavenly places (Ephesians 2:6). After we have been born again or from above, we are placed in Christ and then deployed to the church. The Scriptures declare that the Lord added to the church daily those who were being saved (Acts 2:47).

While the church is not the kingdom and the kingdom is not the church, the church is instrumental to the kingdom. Kingdom citizens have been given the responsibility of holding the keys to the kingdom. When people get saved and are added to the church, it is their responsibility to share the message of the kingdom with non-believers, or the unsaved, so that they may come to Christ. When people share the gospel of the kingdom with those who are not believers, they embrace the message of the kingdom and invite Christ into their hearts as Lord and Savior. Their connection to the church, which is the embassy of God, is accomplished through water baptism, which is an outward representation of an inward salvific experience: that they met Christ, saw and entered the kingdom, and no longer had a primary allegiance to this world but rather to the kingdom of God. The church is responsible for public baptizing, and officers of the church have been granted the authority to baptize. Thus, Phillip baptized the Ethiopian eunuch.

You may be asking, what happened to the church's role within the kingdom? This is a very logical question that any serious Bible student and kingdom citizen would want to know the answer. I will address the church's relationship with the kingdom today in the remainder of this chapter and in the dispensational discussion in the next chapter.

The Church in Transition

Things in the church were kingdom functional for the first three centuries, even though the church was constantly under persecution from both the Jews and the Gentiles. The church was the physical institution, organism, or entity of the kingdom of God—the kingdom command post here on the earth. The church was staffed with fivefold ministry gifts, who were responsible for overseeing the functions of the New Testament church as it executed its role in the kingdom (Ephesians 4:11). There was no such thing as credible rogue citizens of the kingdom. Everyone who was a part of the kingdom movement of Christ was also connected to the formal structure of the church, which ensured that the kingdom culture was being lived out according to the message of Christ. The church was endeavoring to live out the kingdom mandate while ducking and dodging to get the message of the kingdom out and opening new churches in both new and existing territories.

The church was born on Pentecost, continues until today, and will be absorbed in the rapture. The church age ends at the rapture, which is the end of the seven churches of Asia Minor; thus, the church has both an existential and eschatological function. In essence, the churches in Asia Minor were going through certain things during the time of the writing of the book of Revelation, but when you look closer at these seven churches, they are loaded with both historical implications as well as prophetic insight. These seven churches also represent, according to biblical numerology, "completion" for the church. The number seven is the number of completion, maturity, and perfection. If you desire to learn a little more concerning the seven churches of Asia Minor and each book's prophetic insight, I have more detailed information about the seven churches of Asia Minor and their prophetic future in my book, *The Doors of the Church Are Closed.*

So now to answer the question of what happened to the church. Why did it stop doing what it was doing? To answer this question, I want to take a brief look at the major periods of the church. The first section I want to tersely discuss segues us into the four greatest hindrances of the church.

Major Periods of the Church

The early church is covered throughout the book of Acts and represents the church when it was in full kingdom throttle. The church saw itself as the official representative of the kingdom (embassy) and embraced its charge to preach the gospel of the kingdom and preach Jesus as the only way to the kingdom. Functionally, this was the most "kingdom" the church has been historically. The leaders of the church had been personally discipled by Jesus Himself, thus the apostles led the initial church, and those whom they consecrated were the later fivefold officers, elders, and deacons in the Lord's church. The early church experienced persecution from the Jews immediately after its inception and continued to suffer after the destruction of Rome and the temple. The Emperor Nero and other Roman leaders also persecuted the Christian church with no good reason, except being led and controlled by the power of Satan.

The next major era of the church was the cessation of Christian persecution with the signing of the Edict of Milan. Constantine the Great ordered the cessation of Christian persecution in 313 AD, and this began the era of the open or the public church. The church was allowed to come out of the closet. This era provided both positive and negative effects for the Christian church. During this period of time, the church became the official religion of the Roman Empire, and those in the empires could now freely practice Christianity without consequences. However, Christian freedom allowed the church to focus on its theology, ecclesiology, and eschatology as well as creating ecclesiastical councils, which allowed theologians to argue and debate orthodox Christianity. This period also allowed the church to canonize the New Testament and combine it with the Old Testament (397 AD).

However, while this period allowed the church to define its theological beliefs, there were many non-biblical beliefs and practices that were adopted by the Christian church from the polytheistic and pagan practices of the Roman Empire. This era is known as the pagan church because the church in the fourth century adopted many of the pagan temple practices and just renamed them with Christian titles. This was the beginning of redefining the church from a Roman perspective and ignoring its Jewish background. Christianity was birthed out of Judaism; Jesus was a Jew, and He practiced Judaism. Judaism is so important to how we see the church and understand the kingdom that without that knowledge, one cannot understand the New Testament culture. Unfortunately, the Christian church became politicized and was allowed to freely practice this new form of Christianity that had very little interest in the kingdom of God upon the earth. It was more concerned about the Roman Empire now rather than the kingdom in eternity.

The Roman Empire adopted Christianity as its formal religion, integrated it into its governmental practices, and granted its leaders political influence. The church was no longer preoccupied with the kingdom of God; they were now enjoying the opportunity to practice their faith—even if it was a watered down, compromised version of it. However, not all believers were comfortable with the new practices of the faith, and this led to the Monastic Movement. The Monastic Movement was a movement that rejected the new religious freedoms that were infused with pagan practices and worship. This movement gave way to a group of men referred to as monks. Monasticism is from the Greek *monachos* (μοναχός), derived from *monos* (μόνος), which means "alone." Monkhood is a religious way of life in which one renounces worldly pursuits to devote oneself fully to spiritual work. The Monastic Movement saw embracing the Roman culture as embracing a life of ungodliness; St. Augustine was a monk, Martin Luther was an Augustinian monk, etc.

The church had become so secular in its practices and beliefs that many saw no distinction between those who practiced the faith and those who did not. Thus, many early Christians moved to the desert to draw closer to God; many believed this was based upon Christ's example when He went to the wilderness of Judea to fast for 40 days and nights. The words "monk," "monastery," and "monasticism" do not appear in the Bible[5]; these terms simply speak to the separate lives that some chose to live during the creation of the church in Rome. Historically, there have been four waves of monastics: Desert Fathers, Monasteries, Friars, and New Monasticism. Monasticism was a common practice during the persecution and the merging of the church and Rome.

Let's look at what really happened to the kingdom function of the church through four lenses, which are probably, in my estimation, the four greatest hindrances to understanding and experiencing the kingdom. There are four dispensations, or periods of enculturation, that greatly impacted the church and changed its purpose and practice. These four hindrances are:

1. **Romanization:** What is Romanization? Romanization was the removal of Christianity's Jewish background and culture from the church, redefining it with a Roman cultural perspective. During the fourth century, the church became more Roman and its Jewish history was erased. In addition, the church became anti-Semitic, pitching Christianity against

---

[5] Prayerfoundation.org, "Brief History of Christian Monasticism," Retrieved from http://prayerfoundation.org/brief_history_of_christian_monasticism.htm.

Jewish people because of their involvement in the crucifixion of Christ. They blamed the Jews, who rejected Christ as the Messiah, for His death and crucifixion. The Roman Empire totally redefined Christianity from a Roman pagan perspective. This was a tragic series of events that happened over the centuries, because the understanding of the Jewish Messianic expectation of the King of the Jews was the theology upon which the kingdom of God was built. Thus, in order to understand the kingdom, one must have a high regard and respect for Jewish practices and Jewish literature. However, during this period, the Roman Church redefined itself based upon pagan values, beliefs, and culture. The kingdom-focused church that was rooted in Jewish practices and beliefs had faded, and the Roman church was elevated. The Roman Church replaced the kingdom emphasis with a church emphasis and built basilicas throughout the Roman Empire, which were church buildings that attempted to take the form of a temple. This was the first major hindrance to the church, embracing her role as the embassy of the kingdom and taking upon herself the responsibility of spreading the message of the kingdom of God.

2. **Europeanization:** The next major hindrance to the church assuming her functional kingdom role is the era I refer to as Europeanization. Europeanization was the period of time when Christianity was whitewashed and hijacked as the faith of the Europeans. This era gave rise to the Vatican and the Roman Catholic Church and its worldwide political and economic influence. This church movement was responsible for making biblical characters look European, including Jesus. Biblical figures were given European images and contexts, thus Europeans were also seen as superior to other ethnic groups. This caricature benefitted the pope and other top church leaders who were European and gave rise to continued anti-Semitism and the like. This era did not lend itself to a Jewish Jesus nor the focus of the kingdom of God;

instead, Christianity was used as a political showpiece that validated the Roman government and financial corruption.

3. **Colonization:** The next major hindrance that prevented the church from functioning in its role as the kingdom of God was colonization, which brought Protestantism with it. The West and European countries had now embarked upon one of the most hideous crimes of humanity—African slavery. Religion became an important factor in the equation in the spread of slavery as Great Britain and France desired to take over the world and govern it for economic and political power. Both the Protestant church and the Roman Catholic Church financially supported and blessed colonizing efforts. The Society of the Promulgation of the Gospel in Foreign Parts was tasked with placing Protestant churches in the countries that they colonized or to which they had access. This movement affirmed slavery and its practice in the name of God and helped to create a socialized church that had no focus upon the kingdom and its agenda of kingdom discipleship. Colonization proved that believers chose economics over evangelism. This church had long strayed from its Jewish roots, had become racially deceived, and was far from the message of the kingdom of God.

4. **Westernization:** The last major hindrance of the church in embracing a functional kingdom role is Westernization. Westernization took on the form of Western superiority, especially when it came to Africa. Westernization intentionally degraded the role of Africa in Christianity and the Bible. Christianity in the West bought into and adopted Romanization, Europeanization, and colonization. With religion as its backbone, Westernization defined people through the lens of slavery. Thus, the church became stratified based upon race and class, totally ignoring scriptures that stated otherwise. The kingdom message and the kingdom movement were absent from the great theological minds in Germany, England, and America.

The focus of Christianity was based upon a social gospel that affirmed one group of Gentiles over another group of Gentiles, when the scripture says to the Jew first and then the Gentile (Romans 1:16).

The church lost her way throughout history; however, God is sovereign and omniscient, and He always brings us back to where we need to be—the kingdom! Christianity is supposed to be a Judeo-Christian belief that is tied directly to the biblical practices of the great fathers of the faith—Abraham, Isaac, Jacob, and other great Jewish men in our Christian heritage. Many of the church practices we hold dear today do not resemble Christianity in the early church—the church for which Jesus Christ died. As you continue reading this book, prayerfully you will understand what it means to be a kingdom citizen who serves in the church.

Chapter Two
The Seven Dispensations of Theological Renewal and the Kingdom

M Y POSITION CONCERNING THE day and time we live in is that humanity is in the final stage of our understanding of God. We are currently living in the dispensation of the church age or the dispensation of grace. However, within the church age, our understanding of God has progressed dispensationally in thought as well. The church has forgotten its reason for being and is no longer engaged in kingdom business, as discussed earlier. As a result, the contemporary church has lost her way, and the effects of the drift are evident; research suggests that between 8,000 and 10,000 churches are closing annually in America. What is happening with the contemporary church, and why is the attrition rate so high? I believe it is due to two reasons: the rise of the church of Laodicea mentioned in Revelation chapter 3 and the absence of the preaching of the gospel of the kingdom of God.

> *"I know your works, that you are neither cold nor hot. I could wish you were cold or hot. So then, because you are lukewarm, and neither cold nor hot, I will vomit you out of My mouth. Because you say, 'I am rich, have become wealthy, and have need of nothing'—and do not know that you are wretched, miserable, poor, blind, and naked—I counsel you to buy from Me gold refined in the fire, that you*

may be rich; and white garments, that you may be clothed, that the shame of your nakedness may not be revealed; and anoint your eyes with eye salve, that you may see. As many as I love, I rebuke and chasten. Therefore be zealous and repent. Behold, I stand at the door and knock. If anyone hears My voice and opens the door, I will come in to him and dine with him, and he with Me. To him who overcomes I will grant to sit with Me on My throne, as I also overcame and sat down with My Father on His throne."[6]

And this gospel of the kingdom will be preached in all the world as a witness to all the nations, and then the end will come.[7]

The Bible prophesied about the gospel of the kingdom being preached in Matthew 24:14; however, until the 21st century, we have not heard a great deal about it, although a few men over the last few decades wrote some works about it, but not with any substantial change to the local churches' theology. Most churches lacked the understanding and exposure to the concepts of the kingdom of God. Even though men and women of God in academia have known and written about the kingdom of God, instruction in kingdom doctrine has only occurred in churches recently. According to the prophetic clock of God, the time is now—it's time for a kingdom reformation!

We have taken a light look at the church versus the kingdom and the church historically. We now want to take a look at the church historically from a doctrinal perspective. By examining the changes in Christian doctrine through the prism of dispensation, we can again see how the church has departed from its original intent and the message of the kingdom of God. For this cause, I developed Seven Dispensations of Theological Renewal:

---

[6] Revelation 3:15–21 (NKJV).

[7] Matthew 24:14 (NKJV).

1. Revelation
2. Identification
3. Salvation
4. Regeneration
5. Impartation
6. Participation
7. Exaltation

We will look at the church's teachings through these seven epochs of time:

The Dispensation of Revelation

The early church was given the most comprehensive understanding of the gospel of the kingdom and the mission of Christ. The early church gleaned from eyewitnesses and the apostles on the proper way to live for Christ. The disciples were extremely important in ensuring that the message that they had heard and seen was spread throughout the world. The disciples were not operating out of hearsay; they were actual eyewitnesses who experienced the ministry of Jesus firsthand and who were trained by Jesus Himself (Acts 4:20). The early church not only benefited from the teachings of the disciples, but the Gentiles did as well; the apostles presided on the Jerusalem Council concerning the integration of the Gentiles. The early church represents the most powerful representation of the call and cause of Christ that we know of. The gospels give us detailed narratives of the life, mission, and teachings of Christ, as witnessed by His disciples. The book of Acts demonstrates how the disciples (later the apostles) executed what Christ commissioned them to do for His kingdom. Thus, the gospels and the book of Acts serve as a historical record of the intended focus and scope of the mission of the church and its teachings.

I refer to this era as the Dispensation of Revelation because this was the era in which the Holy Spirit revealed that which was not known to the inspired men who wrote the Word of God. I want to make sure I emphasize the preeminence of the Word of God. The Bible was not given to us by interpretation, so it has no errors. Men, assigned to provide the world with the Word of God, penned the Bible through God-breathed inspiration (2 Timothy 3:16). If anyone had or any era contained a holistic understanding of the Word of God, it was the first century saints and the early church. The early church was the first and only dispensation in which the mind of God was understood concerning His kingdom, the church, and the world. The time span for the early church occurred from Pentecost through the third century. This church actually laid the foundation for the gospel to be preached upon every continent. This church witnessed to the excellency of Christ from Jerusalem to the uttermost parts of the world! Its members understood their mission, their methodology, their mandate, and their message! The early church was persecuted for its faith, was dispersed, and its leaders became martyrs for the faith.

The Dispensation of Identification

This dispensation was both a blessing and a cursing. This dispensation was birthed in the fourth century upon the cessation of Christian persecution with the signing of the Edict of Milan. This official document ended Christian persecution and allowed Christians to freely practice their faith. During this era, Christianity became the official religion of the Roman Empire. That's right—to be a Roman citizen was to be a Christian and to be a Christian was to be a Roman citizen. To be Roman and Christian was synonymous in nomenclature. With the freedom to practice Christianity, void of the fear and threat of persecution and death, the church could now attend to its unfinished business. However, since Christianity had become the official religion of Rome, there was no need for the church to fulfill the Great Commission. The entire Roman Empire was automatically Christian and baptized as infants into the faith. This era opened the doors of the church! The Roman Empire, led by the influence of Constantine the Great, opened the doors of the church, and everyone became a member. Conversion was unnecessary in this new Christian religion as long as you were a citizen or member of the Roman Empire. The empire thought that one of the highest privileges the church could have ever been given was Roman legitimacy since the Roman Empire was believed to be one of the most advanced and superior empires in the world, but this marriage between the state and the church would haunt the Christian church forever!

The blessing that came out of this era was the peace and tranquility the church experienced that allowed for the collection of all the writings of the apostles. Those men gathered in 397 AD at the Council of Carthage, inspired to compile, copy, and translate the Bible. Prior to collecting all of the writings, this era was famously known for its church doctrine councils. These councils were designed to decide what would be the official doctrines of Christianity and would convene and rigorously argue and debate scripture and theological themes. Many of the most renowned theological thinkers, commonly referred to as the patristics or early church fathers, emerged from these councils. Many of them, originating from Northern Africa, became known for developing the primary doctrines of the church, formally named church creeds. Some of the most important creeds that came out of these councils were the Nicene Creed, the Constantinople Creed, the Athanasian Creed, and the Apostles' Creed. Also among these councils were Chalcedon and Ephesus, who were very instrumental during the Dispensation of Identification.

Why do I refer this era as the Dispensation of Identification? The Dispensation of Identification allowed the church to fully identify who Christ was in relationship to God the Father and God the Holy Spirit. During this era, Christ was declared *homoousia*, or of the "same substance as God." After careful study of the Scriptures, Christ was declared fully God and fully man while not confounding or mixing the two natures of Christ. This is the dispensation wherein we identified who God is in relationship to His triune presentation—one God in three Persons. Our present-day understanding of Christ as both Lord and Savior and God and man developed during this era. This era was also marked by such great thinkers as Athanasius, St. Augustine, Origen, Tertullian, Chrysostom, Cyprian, the three Cappadocians, and others. This era extended from the fourth century through the 16th century. Consider this: For the first 16 centuries minus the early church, the only revelation the church had was the identity of God.

The Dispensation of Salvation

This era, beginning in the 1500s, is called the pre-Reformation movement. During this period, the theology of the Roman Catholic Church was beginning to be challenged by men such as John Wycliffe and John Huss. The Reformation period culminated under the efforts of Martin Luther, who had an experience that caused him to re-examine the Scriptures concerning what the church taught about eternal life and how one obtains eternal life. Luther disagreed with the extra measures the church required people to perform in order to be in right standing with God and please Him (works righteousness). Luther's research led him to conclude that salvation cannot be granted by the Roman Catholic Church or through penance or prayers for the dead. Luther concluded that the only way one could have eternal life was through four Latin phrases: *sola fide, sola gratia, sola scriptura,* and *solus Christos* (by faith alone, by grace alone, by scripture alone, and by Christ alone). Luther challenged Roman Catholic scholars to an open theological debate concerning salvation by nailing his 95 Theses, or statements against the theology of the Roman Catholic Church, on the door of the church in Wittenberg, Germany. His theses condemned their teachings. Of course, that did not go over very well, and Luther never got a chance to debate his positions but had to be hurried out of the city and placed in hiding. Luther was a wanted man for concluding that you did not need to embrace the traditions of the

Roman Catholic Church in order to have a relationship with Christ. He stated that in order to be saved or have a relationship with God, only faith, grace, scripture, and Christ were required. Luther was not attempting to shut the doors of the Roman Catholic Church; he was simply challenging the church to rethink its teaching.

The reason I refer to this dispensation as the Dispensation of Salvation is because Luther's treatises serve as the basis for our soteriology, or doctrine of salvation. Luther was not a lone ranger in this endeavor—men such as John Calvin and Ulrich Zwingli also challenged Roman Catholicism and its lack of biblical basis for its beliefs and practices. The Dispensation of Salvation covered the 1500s and the 1600s. Wow! Consider this—we are in the 1600s, and the only thing we know about God is who He is and the requirements of salvation.

The Dispensation of Regeneration

This dispensation has its roots in the English Reformation. The study of English Protestantism and Roman Catholicism is a very interesting historical investigation for those of you who enjoy soap operas. The official religion of England depended upon which king or queen was in office. The changing of the guard was always accompanied with drama. However, one of the greatest reformers and preachers who ever lived came out of this era in the 1700s, a man by the name of John Wesley. Wesley was a tremendous preacher and has been called the father of the Methodist church. He was an itinerant preacher who traveled around the country preaching the gospel. He could have been what some would refer to as a fire and brimstone preacher. His message focused upon regeneration, and he was instrumental in reinstituting the message of regeneration in the church. He boldly proclaimed, "You must be born again!"

He and his brother, Charles Wesley, along with other powerful English preachers throughout two centuries, were instrumental in heralding the message of regeneration. John and Charles Wesley, George Whitefield, and others were also instrumental in influencing religious groups like the Quakers and the Puritans toward religious pietism. Wesley focused upon ensuring that people had the internal witness of the Spirit of God to confirm that they were a child of God. I refer to this as the Dispensation of Regeneration because the message of conversion was preached and embraced in the 18th and 19th centuries. Wesley stressed the spiritual experience; he saw the need for believers to have two encounters with God—salvation and perfect love—because both were acts of grace. Wesley's fervor earned him the title of the primary founder of the "you-must-be-born-again" movement. This is also referred to as the Great Awakening or the revivalist era (Jonathan Edwards, George Whitefield, John and Charles Wesley, D.L. Moody, Charles Spurgeon, etc., in England, Scotland, and America). In America, the Great Awakening period produced the message of rejuvenation and gave birth to the first black Baptist church in mid-18th century America: Silver Bluff Baptist Church of Aiken County, South Carolina.

Let's review for a moment: Here we are in the 1700s to the 1900s, and the only things that we have regained and recaptured from the early church so far is who God is, how one is saved, and how, in order to be saved, one must be born again. As you can see, one of the reasons the church is crippled and its members are ignorant and trapped inside is due to its need for theological renewal. We left the doctrine of the early church and have been poisoned through the opened doors of the church that have allowed everything in and out!

The Dispensation of Impartation

This is the dispensation of what has been called the baptism of the Holy Spirit, evidenced by glossolalic speech, or "tongues." This dispensation was an extremely important dispensation marked by the number five (as the fifth dispensation), which is the number of grace. This dispensation gave birth to the revisitation of the Holy

Spirit. While this dispensation probably represents one of the most controversial dispensations within the Protestant Movement, it served as the catalyst for worldwide ministry. The baptism in the Holy Spirit was the dispensation in which the Spirit came to help us unify and to empower God's people for service. However, due to racism in America and the lack of sound biblical doctrine, the movement was minimized in America while having worldwide effects abroad. This movement took place during a time when one of the most heretical theological works (although heralded as one of the most scholarly works of the ages) was published: *The Negro: A Beast or in the Image of God* by Professor C. Carroll. His work was launched as a scientific and theological project that would educate Americans about the place of Negros in America. He stated that blacks belong to the animal kingdom of beasts and were created on the fifth day. He said that Negroes were pre-Adamites.

At the same time, God sent an overabundance of His Spirit to a group of people worshipping on Azusa St. in California. The Holy Spirit ignited His people for ministry but to no avail. Racism and hatred were too prominent for whites to identify with blacks, even in the church. Society deemed the entire movement heretical. The main reason the movement was highly rejected was because its leader was a one-eyed black man named William J. Seymour. Seymour received the teaching for this experience from a white gentleman by the name of William Parham. Historians suggest that Parham, who was a KKK sympathizer, never experienced glossolalic speech. The Holy Spirit was first believed to have fallen upon one of Parham's students, Agnes Ozman. After reports spread of the Holy Spirit falling upon the house church in which Seymour pastored, the movement began to catch the attention of the world.

The Holy Spirit fell heavily upon those services, and people not only spoke in other tongues, but other manifestations occurred on Bonnie Brea St. The movement later spread to Azusa St., and as the young people say, it was off the chain. People were experiencing the baptism of the Holy Spirit for the empowerment of service and the unification of God's people. Unfortunately, the movement did not unite God's people but further divided them along the lines of race and class. The movement slowly began to be identified with the rigidity of the Holiness Movement and the classism of the Assemblies of God.

This movement was pivotal and continues today as the most vital and vibrant aspect of the Body of Christ. This experience has crossed denominational lines, racial lines, and geographical lines. The baptism in the Holy Spirit is a global movement of the Spirit. The normative experience of speaking in other tongues in the early church was not known in our contemporary context until the 1800s in Great Britain under the leadership of Edward Irving and the Catholic Apostolic Church of Scotland and then later the United States on Azusa St. Beloved, it took us until the 20th century to come to know the following: who God is, how one is saved, that you must be born again, and how one is empowered for service. In the Dispensation of Impartation, we learned the necessity of the power of the Holy Spirit for Christian service.

The Dispensation of Participation

This era covers what has been called the Pentecostal/Charismatic/Full Gospel Movements. These movements have been instrumental in laying the foundation for laymen engaging in their faith and participating in worship. This movement gave birth to prayer ministries, such as "Can ye not tarry for one hour?" by Dr. Larry Lea. This dispensation gave rise to an emphasis on studying the scriptures and trusting God according to His Word. During this era, teachings on spiritual warfare and seed sowing for ministry began. This dispensation is responsible for the Praise and Worship Movement that created a new genre of interactive music, praise dancing, and the integration of the fine arts in worship. In biblical numerology, six is the number of man. The sixth dispensation of theological renewal was the dispensation wherein man was now an active participant in worship. This aspect of the church was something totally different from Catholicism and the mainline churches and was revolutionary in the European church world. The sixth dispensation was the era in which men were allowed to express their faith and the formality of religion was subtly abandoned. The need for formally trained clergy diminished, and an emphasis on Bible training was traded for experience. This is the era when people stopped saying, "The Bible states…" and exchanged biblical authority for spiritual experience. The new statements were "The Spirit said to me…" and "The Holy Ghost taught me…." Laymen no longer demanded that their leaders be trained in the Word, and denominations, who demanded trained leaders, declined. So this dispensation has produced a generation of ignorant pulpits: men and women who taught simply from inspiration, totally devoid of information through education.

This era became not only a dispensation wherein man engaged his faith but also went to extremes to the point of no biblical accountability and a subsequent rise in pride/insecurity, arrogance, and spiritual deception due to a lack of a firm theological education. This is the era in which the blind began to lead the blind. Please don't get me wrong: Everyone does not have to go to seminary, but everyone who is called to pastor or preach must sit under someone who has been trained at some level in properly interpreting the Word of God. Even Paul, who knew the Law, prepared for an additional three years (some say with Jesus Himself) after his conversion and call before he began his ministry for Christ.

Let's recap the dispensations before we go on to what I call the last dispensation of theological renewal:

1. **Revelation:** The Early Church (Comprehensive understanding of the Mission, Mandate, Methodology, and Message of Christ and His Kingdom)
2. **Identification:** The Roman Empire/Imperial Church (Who is Christ in relationship to the Triune God and man?)

3. **Salvation:** The Reformation (How is one saved?)
4. **Regeneration:** The Great Awakening (You must be born again.)
5. **Impartation:** The Azusa Outpouring (Empowerment for service and unity)
6. **Participation:** The Pentecostal/Charismatic/Full Gospel Movements (Engaging one's faith at every level)

The Dispensation of Exaltation

This is the Dispensation of the kingdom of God. When you review how long it has taken us to recapture what the first century knew and practiced, it is simply amazing. From the fourth century to the 21st century, believers were finally challenged to focus upon the proclamation, explanation, and demonstration of the kingdom of God—the things Christ focused upon when He was here. This is the dispensation wherein truly Spirit-filled people will abandon the banner of traditionalism and church, which is rooted in the sociological whims of a racist, classist, and heretical church. Even though the Bible is referenced, the basis for its beliefs and teachings of the sociological church are not biblical. Christ has a people who will come out from those who have a form of godliness but deny the power—the church of Laodicea. Paul admonished Timothy to stay away from them (2 Timothy 3:5). There are people who have learned to enjoy church without Christ, and they have been doing it so long that they no longer have the ability to recognize that He is no longer present in the building (Revelation 3:20).

Through a process, the church of Laodicea put Christ out of the church. The process involved the following:

- The exaltation of culture
- The exaltation of class
- The exaltation of cause

When the church placed cultural preferences above kingdom culture, the church invited Christ to exit. After that, the church categorized people according to their class, thus asking for the Christ-founded egalitarian scale (how you measure someone's value) to be abandoned. The church further exemplified the lack of the need for the affirmation of Christ. Then, the last thing that finally put Him out was when the church rallied its own causes and not the cause of Christ. Thus, the Great Commission was exchanged for financial commissions and personal commission (a better you).

The seventh dispensation will focus upon the proclamation of the kingdom of God as a witness and then the end of the church age. Its mission is to bring people to Christ and His kingdom and invite people out of the closed doors of the church. In this dispensation, the church will learn more about the kingdom and walk in kingdom power and authority, literally snatching souls out of the snares of the enemy. This is also an era in which you must be careful because men have already begun changing the kingdom message to lift the authority of man and not God. In the kingdom, God is sovereign, and we are His faithful servants. His kingdom does not reflect a British or Chinese kingdom; His kingdom is a biblical kingdom wherein He alone sits on the throne as the one true King. Be careful when men tell you the King has to get your permission to act.

In God's kingdom, His subjects die daily to their flesh and live daily for His kingdom. This is the opposite of what the church of Laodicea is characterized for; their testimony is "We are rich in increase, have become wealthy, and have need of nothing!" Notice that this church is a church that focuses upon its confession of wealth, for the text states, "For you say!" It is a church that seeks after riches and material gain. It is a church that prioritizes increase. You cannot listen to Christian TV without hearing one of those three Laodicean messages:

1) Watch your confession.
2) You are called to be a millionaire, so make a switch to rich.
3) By the covenant of Abraham, expect an increase.

Now don't get me wrong, who doesn't desire to have his needs taken care of in abundance? The problem is not money—it is focus! Subscription to this philosophy means believing God for material things while ignoring the salvation of thousands daily. The Bible states that God added to the church daily. I wonder how many souls are ignored while men seek increase.

Beloved, we must listen attentively for the voice of God as revealed in His Word. As mentioned earlier, it is very difficult to decipher between the Word of God and the traditions of men because when the doors of the church were opened by Constantine and widened by the Church of England and the American church system, all kinds of things came in. A lot of what came in the church was taught as the revelation of God but was nothing more than the culture of men.

Chapter Three
Jesus and the Kingdom

NOW THAT WE HAVE discussed the distinction between the church and the kingdom, as well as the role of the church as it relates to the kingdom in light of the seven dispensations, let's dig in and talk straight kingdom. The discussion of any kingdom begins with a king, and the King of the kingdom of God is Jesus. Three components go into establishing a kingdom. Those components are as follows:

What Makes Up a Kingdom?		
Component	Definition	Scripture Reference
King	One who rules with authority	John 1:49
Realm	The kingdom proper—its natural parameters and geography	Matthew 6:10
Subjects	Citizens	Ephesians 2:19, Philippians 3:20

King

In a kingdom, there is only one who has ultimate authority, and that is the king. In the kingdom of God, Christ is the reigning ruler. He is the one true King!

Subjects

A kingdom consists of citizens who are born into it (John 3:3–5, Philippians 3:20, Ephesians 2:19). Romans 10:9–10 states the following:

> *"that if you confess with your mouth the Lord Jesus and believe in your heart that God has raised Him from the dead, you will be saved. For with the heart one believes unto righteousness, and with the mouth confession is made unto salvation."*

Thus, the heartfelt belief in and confession of Christ as Lord is the means by which admittance to God's kingdom is obtained.

Realm

Christ is the King of God's kingdom, and the realm over which He has been granted divine rule and authority is the whole earth and everything within it.[8] His realm is also manifested in the hearts of the men and women who subject themselves to His rule and seek His throne for their deliverance (salvation). When it comes to the King's kingdom, the Bible states that the earth is the Lord's and the fullness thereof (Psalm 24:1); however, Jesus, while He was here on Earth, said that His kingdom was not of this world (John 18:36). Which one is it? While God is the Creator and upholder of the world, it is very clear that the earth does not yield to God's rule and reign. The kingdom is present in the world but not in totality. The Bible informs us that Satan is the god of this world (2 Corinthians 4:4), and all that is in this world is the lust of the flesh, the lust of the eyes, and the pride of life (1 John 2:16).

---

[8] BeHealedToday, "God's Kingdom Is Here," Retrieved from https://sites.google.com/site/behealedtoday/home.

There are clearly two kingdoms in conflict: God's kingdom versus Satan's kingdom. However, just because evil rules on the earth does not mean that God does not own the world. It simply means that God's rule and reign have yet to be fully established upon the earth. God's kingdom came to turn this world upside down by overturning Satan's kingdom power and influence. Any time we see the works of Satan overturned, we are looking at the kingdom of God. In order for God to possess something, this does not mean that He has to govern it. A good example of this is the soul of man: God says in Ezekiel 18:4, "Behold, all souls are Mine; the soul of the father as well as the soul of the son is Mine; the soul who sins shall die." Even though God claims total ownership of every soul, He does not rule and reign in every soul's life. Giving us free moral agency, He allows us to choose to let Him reign or not reign in our lives.

Another way to understand the kingdom of God is that a kingdom is comprised of a king, his court, and a territory. The kingdom of God, being a proper kingdom, has each of these:

- **A king who rules with authority** – You must have a king who has a domain or dominion, and this king must rule with authority. The King of our kingdom is the Lord, and His domain is the whole earth, heaven, and all who dwell within.
- **A king's court** – The king has to have a cabinet of people who represent Him abroad. The court of the Lord's kingdom is comprised of His fivefold ministry leaders that He has called to hold office in His church.
- **A territory** – In order for there to be a kingdom, a king has to have a territory, an area over which he reigns. As the eternal King, God's territory is currently the believer.

Yet another way of understanding God's kingdom is acknowledging that every kingdom has four basic components:

1. A ruler or who rules

2. Subjects
3. A domain or geography of rulership
4. Laws

The kingdom of God has these four basic components:

1. God is the King.
2. We are His subjects.
3. His domain is our hearts and wherever we are situated or established. Wherever we go, we bring the kingdom. God rules and reigns wherever we are and wherever He plants us!
4. Christ is the ruler who reigns from heaven for eternity in the hearts of His subjects and governs them by the Word of God.

So exactly who is Jesus? Where did He come from? How is He related to David? What makes Him King? And what was His message? As we discuss Jesus and the kingdom, it is my desire to answer these five questions while communicating the ministry focus and message of Jesus.

Jesus, according to scripture, is the Son of God. The Bible teaches us that Christ was the one of a kind (only begotten) Son of God, according to John 3:16. The Bible teaches us that Jesus is also the fulfillment of prophecy. According to John 1:1, Jesus was the Word of God, and according to John 1:14, He became flesh and dwelled among us. Jesus was the incarnate Word of God that took flesh upon Himself (Philippians 2:7–10) and became a man. God is His Father, and Mary was His mother. However, Jesus was virgin born; Mary was impregnated by the Seed of God through the Holy Spirit, void of a physical, sexual encounter because she received the Seed of God by faith (Luke 1:38). Jesus was the prophetic fulfillment of the prophecies of Isaiah and other prophets. Isaiah actually prophesied the virgin birth in Isaiah 7:14 and 9:6–7. According to Jewish culture, it was the role of the father to name the child, and when you read scripture, you discover that Joseph did not name Jesus but God the Father named Him (Matthew 1:18–25).

Jesus came through the line of David; Matthew recorded 42 generations to ensure that the Jewish roots of Jesus were established and that He was in the bloodline of David, which qualified Him for prophetic fulfillment. Jesus was the anticipated Messiah, the King of the Jews. Jesus was both an Old Testament fulfillment of prophecy as well as an intertestamental expectation. When Jesus came, Paul writes that it was the fullness of time when God sent forth His Son, born of a woman, under the Jewish law. This chapter is not designed to be a Christological chapter focusing upon Christ being fully God and fully man; however, I just want to state the fact that Jesus was and is the eternal Son of God who is the king of the kingdom of God. Jesus is He who now sits upon the throne of David, and His government will have no end.

The Bible provides us with narratives concerning His birth to toddlerhood. Later, when He was 12, we see Him in the Temple teaching, and then when He was 30, He began His Galilean ministry. When He was born, the wise men stated that He was the one who was born King of the Jews (Matthew 2:2). It was the fact that Christ was thought to be the expected Messiah and King of the Jews that sent Herod into hysterics. When Pilate asked Jesus if He was King, Jesus' response was "You have said rightly…" Jesus acknowledged that He was a king, but His kingdom was not of this world (John 18:36–37). Against the wishes of the Jews, Pilate wrote an inscription that Jesus was King of the Jews and placed it on His cross. It is clear that Jesus' focus was the kingdom of God. Not only was He the King of the Jews, but He is the King of a universal kingdom that all people, regardless of their ethnicity or religious backgrounds, can gain entry to if they will confess Him as Lord and Savior and believe in the power of His death, burial, and resurrection (Romans 10:8–10).

Let's now look at the ministry focus of Jesus. The first stirrings of a revival of the kingdom theme in Jewish culture occurred some 400 years after the writings of the Prophet Malachi, when John the Baptist (better described as John the baptizing one) appeared in the Jordan region trumpeting a peculiar message in the wilderness. John provided us with an appetizer for the ministry of Jesus by preaching that the kingdom of heaven is at hand—so repent! Before we move on, I do want to point out that the kingdom of God is the same thing as the kingdom of heaven. "Heaven" is used instead of "God" simply to avoid the use of the sacred name of "God," but they both refer to His kingdom. Some people get confused when they start studying the kingdom in scripture because they see both the "kingdom of heaven" and the "kingdom of God" used in scripture. The reason for this can be explained by the concept of circumlocution, which simply means other ways to refer to God without using the name of God. There is no difference between the kingdom of God and the kingdom of heaven. It is the same reality spoken of differently. Matthew used kingdom of heaven, and Mark and Luke tended to use kingdom of God. A few times Matthew used the kingdom of God, but for the most part, he used kingdom of heaven in order not to violate reverencing the name of God.

There is a reason for this: Each one of the gospels is written from a different persuasion. Matthew was a Jew and wrote from a Jewish standpoint. Mark and Luke were Gentiles and wrote from a Gentile standpoint. When Matthew wrote of the kingdom, he said, "kingdom of heaven," because he was a Jew, and according to Jewish beliefs, they tried to stay away from using the name of God. In the Old Testament, when the Jews would write the name of God, or Yahweh, they would take the vowels out so that "YHWH" could not be pronounced—they felt the name was sacred. When the vowel markers are taken out, this is called the tetragrammaton. Another way Jews reverenced God's name in their writing was as the scrolls were copied, every time the scribes came to God's name, they would bow and say, *"Ha Shem,"* which means "the name." In many texts, they would even substitute the name *Adonai*, which means "Lord." Thus, Matthew the Jew utilized circumlocution because the Jewish law said that you should not take the name of the Lord in vain. By using "heaven," Matthew avoided using God's name. Whereas Matthew was careful not to violate the name of God, Mark and Luke did not have that same kind of reverence or sensitivity for the name of God, so they used the phrase "kingdom of God" in their writings.

John was considered a forerunner of Christ. John was a voice, not an echo; thus, his message was fresh because he was preaching something that people were not used to hearing. John's mission was to prepare the way for the ministry of Christ by stirring the hearts and minds of people unto repentance in preparation for the ministry of the King (Luke 1:17). The Greek word for "repent" is *metanoeó* [<met-an-o-eh-o> (μετανοέω)], which means "to think differently or afterwards, reconsider, repent, to change one's mind."

For this is he who was spoken of by the prophet Isaiah, saying: "The voice of one crying in the wilderness: 'Prepare the way of the Lord; Make His paths straight.'"[9]

John was the King's heralder, proclaiming the message of the coming of the King. Luke 16:16 and Matthew 11:12–14 both speak of the kingdom as a dispensational manifestation; thus the text states:

> *"The law and the prophets were until John. Since that time the kingdom of God has been preached, and everyone is pressing into it."*[10]

> *And from the days of John the Baptist until now the kingdom of heaven suffers violence, and the violent take it by force.*

---

[9] Matthew 3:3 (NJKV).
[10] Luke 16:16 (NKJV).

> *For all the prophets and the law prophesied until John. And
> if you are willing to receive it, he is Elijah who is to come."[11]*

John is referred to as Elijah in the Matthean text, where Jesus
quotes Malachi 3:1:

> *"Behold, I send My messenger, and he will prepare the way
> before Me. And the Lord, whom you seek, will suddenly come
> to His temple, even the Messenger of the covenant, in whom
> you delight. Behold, He is coming," Says the LORD of hosts.*

John operated by the prophetic clock of God. John's ministry
and message were dispensational; John was the forerunner of the
kingdom movement who advertised and made ready the way for
the people to receive Christ and His kingdom. The role of John
was the following:

- Baptize
- Refer people to Christ
- Resist the present religious movement
- Be sacrificed for the Kingdom Movement

John's message was only to set the stage for Christ, not for himself;
John was not an opportunist, and he recognized his own role. His
message eventually became irrelevant to the cause, as revealed in
Acts 19. John teaches us that our value to the King is rooted in His
ability to use us, and once the King is finished with us, He brings
us home. John the baptizing one served a tremendous purpose in
the kingdom of God; however, the Bible states that he that is least in
the kingdom is greater than John (Matthew 11:11). What a privilege
to be in the kingdom! You are greater than John. He proclaimed
the kingdom now, but he himself was not yet in the kingdom, for
one could not gain access into the kingdom until Christ's death and
resurrection. John was still part of the Old Testament covenant until

---

[11] Matthew 11:12–14 (NKJV).

Christ died and led captivity captive (Ephesians 4:8–10). Christ freed those under the old covenant after His descent to Hades and freed those who died under the Law but experienced grace through Old Testament sacrifices. You are blessed to be in the kingdom, and it is a privilege to be in the kingdom and to be used by God to proclaim the kingdom. Times and seasons are critical, and you and I have been called into the kingdom for such a time as this. A man is great when he can embrace his season, rise to the occasion, and dare to be different. John was different, thus he was greater than all preceding prophets for he was a voice, not an echo. He had a unique season, executed it with class, and was then put to death.

Christ's mission was to:

- Fulfill the Jewish prophesies (born King of the Jews).
- Inaugurate the kingdom (authority over Satan).
- Provide global access to the kingdom (Passover Lamb).
- Empower witnesses (authority over Satanic influence).
- Expand the kingdom message (God's dominion, rule, reign, and realm of influence).

Thus, when Jesus came to Earth, He came preaching the kingdom, not the church (Matthew 4:17, 23). The gospels are inundated with the focus of the kingdom of God. The Bible states that Jesus "went about all the cities and villages, teaching in their synagogues, preaching the gospel of the kingdom, and healing every sickness and every disease among the people" (Matthew 9:35). Thus, Christ engaged His ministry with four focuses:

- **Proclamation (Matthew 4:17)** – The reign of God has drawn near! He made known that the kingdom was available and near them. He also proclaimed His mission, which was to seek and save those that are lost.
- **Explanation (Matthew 4:23)** – The kingdom is like… He went into a deeper explanation of the principles that He

proclaimed by teaching the kingdom, using parables to make the message clearer.

- **Demonstration (Matthew 9:35)** – Christ demonstrated the authority of the kingdom through manifestations of healing, deliverance, etc. He moved in miracles, signs, and wonders to show that the power of God was real and that He had authority over all the power of the enemy.
- **Invitation (Matthew 9:36–38)** – The kingdom is available through belief in Christ. He encouraged people to deny themselves and what they wanted to do and to follow Him instead—to enter the kingdom.

By preaching, Jesus announced the message of the kingdom of God; by teaching, He explained its meaning and character; by healing and miracles, He demonstrated its presence and power in the world.[12] The kingdom of God was clearly the highest order people could aspire to, and becoming a citizen of God's kingdom was the greatest privilege made available to humanity.

Jesus' preaching of the kingdom message was effective because He engaged in an approach that integrated proclaiming the kingdom, teaching people about the kingdom, showing them the power of the kingdom, and then challenging them to be a part of it. Christ lived His life to explain the culture of the kingdom and the necessity of entering the kingdom. During His three-year ministry, Christ taught the following regarding the kingdom of God:

- The kingdom of God is spiritual (John 4:24).
- The kingdom is to be valued above all else (Matthew 13:44–45).
- The kingdom must be sought out (Matthew 6:33)

---

[12] Dr. Trevor Grizzle and Dr. Dana Carson, ed., "The Kingdom in the New Testament." Kingdom Scholar's Handbook (Dana Carson Kingdom Ministries), pp. 18-19.

- You must be born again to see and enter the kingdom (John 3:3–5).
- The kingdom is redemptive and causes men to repent (Matthew 21:32).
- The kingdom is multicultural (Matthew 13:47).
- His kingdom is not of this world (John 18:36).
- The mysteries of the kingdom are privileged information (Mark 4).
- The kingdom is a present and future reality (Matthew 10:5–7, 12:28).

The kingdom was first offered to the Jews and then the Gentiles:

"And I say to you that many will come from east and west, and sit down with Abraham, Isaac, and Jacob in the kingdom of heaven. But the sons of the kingdom will be cast out into outer darkness. There will be weeping and gnashing of teeth."[13]

"Therefore I say to you, the kingdom of God will be taken from you and given to a nation bearing the fruits of it. And whoever falls on this stone will be broken; but on whomever it falls, it will grind him to powder."[14]

John 1 says that He came to His own, but His own did not receive Him, but to them that received Him, to them He gave the right to become the sons of God if they would believe in His name (John 1:12). We, the Gentiles, were allowed access to the kingdom of God because God's original covenant people, the Jews, did not receive Him. This does not mean all the Jews of course, because the first kingdom citizens were Jews. The disciples/apostles were also Jews, and the book of Acts records the active salvation of Jewish people until Acts 8, when the Samaritans were brought into the kingdom.

---

[13] Matthew 8:11–12 (NKJV).
[14] Matthew 21:43–44 (NKJV).

From Acts 10 through the remaining chapters, the Gentile world was under kingdom siege! You and I have been given entrance into the kingdom of God because Israel as a nation, specifically its leaders and those whom they influenced, by the design of God, rejected Christ as King. The Matthean gospel suggests this about the kingdom of God: The Jews did not receive the message of Christ, so it became available to the Gentiles, or non-Jewish people. The Gentiles would be those that would receive Him and call upon Him to be saved.

Jesus came preaching the good news of the kingdom to everyone that would hear His message, revealing how the kingdom functions and how people can gain entrance into the kingdom. It is crystal clear that Jesus' focus was the kingdom of God, and today our churches are focusing on the church and, in many church circles, secular humanism. It is kingdom time, and through the ministry of Jesus, God has made the kingdom of God available to you and me.

When Was the Concept of "Kingdom of God" Created?

When the New Testament opens up, John the baptizing one and others are freely using the terms "kingdom of God" and "kingdom of heaven." But where do these New Testament creations come from? When we close the book of Malachi, we do not hear a clear-cut message of the kingdom. However, as soon as we open up Matthew, there is the kingdom—seemingly out of the blue! The answer is found in the Intertestamental Period, a period of time that is key to understanding Jesus' kingdom message. So what is the Intertestamental Period? The Intertestamental Period is the gap of time between the Old Testament and the New Testament, when dreadful things happened to God's people, including exile and persecution. The concept of the kingdom is what we call an intertestamental development; it emerged during the 400 or so years between these two periods, during which God was "silent"—not silent in the literal sense, but He was silent to them. God, who is the Word, never stops talking, as seen in Hebrews 1:3 and John

1:1. The Intertestamental Period was one of the most horrendous times in history for the Jews.

- The northern kingdom went into Assyrian exile starting in 722 BC.
- The southern kingdom went into Babylonian exile in 586 BC.
- In the 300s, they went into Persian exile, but the Persians allowed them the freedom to practice their faith, worship, and rebuild their temple, which had been destroyed.
- After Persian rule came Hellenization under Alexander the Great, and the Jews were persecuted again. Alexander saw Greek culture as superior and desired to Hellenize the world (in other words, to convert everything under his rule to the Greek language and culture). In light of this, the Jews were prohibited from using Hebrew, and they were prohibited from temple worship. It was also during this time that the Aramaic language developed.

Several groups and traditions developed during the Intertestamental Period. You do not see them in the Old Testament, but as soon as you open up the New Testament, they are present (and if you are really serious about scripture, you should be asking, "Where did these concepts come from, and how did they emerge?"):

- The religious sects like the Sadducees, Pharisees, Essenes, Herodians, Zealots, etc.
- The oral traditions of the rabbis (Mishnah)
- The Day of the Lord – Because the Jews had suffered so much at the hands of their persecutors, the concept developed that one day, there would be a day of destruction of their enemies. On this "Day of the Lord," God would destroy evil and bring in a new regime through which the Jews would have the kingdom restored to them.

- Synagogues – Synagogues were developed during the Intertestamental Period once the temple was destroyed. Synagogues were used primarily for instruction in the Law for all classes of Jews. In order to gather at a synagogue, it was required for Jews to have a minyan, which was a representation of ten men. Once the Jews rebuilt their temple, they kept the synagogue as a place of smaller worship. Thus, they worshiped in the synagogue in addition to worshiping in the temple.

The Day of the Lord developed during the time of the Maccabean Revolt. The Syrian king, who embraced Greek ways, tried to get the Jews to abandon their faith, but instead of doing so, the Jews fought back. After they saw how wicked things had gotten, they began to embrace the belief that God was going to have to develop a whole new reality for them. The theme of "the kingdom of God" emerged because they saw that there were forces of evil fighting against the forces of God. The belief was that when God inaugurated His kingdom on the Day of the Lord, He would overturn the effects of Satan and the fall of man. He would come to fight for His people with great power, signs, and wonders. During the time of their persecution, Antiochus Epiphanes launched a tremendous attack against the Jews and destroyed their temple. This time period was sparked by a macabre time of Jewish persecution and they believed that the world had become too evil to redeem. The Jews believed that there would come a day when God would totally destroy and annihilate evil by sending the Messiah and then turn the world over to the Jews. They believed that when the Messiah would manifest, He would do so with powers that overturned the work of Satan. If you recall, when John the Baptist was in prison questioning Jesus' ministry tactics, Jesus told the disciples to go tell John that the dumb were talking, the blind were receiving their sight, etc. In other words, Jesus was saying to John that these were signs of the manifestation of the kingdom of God. If John could not believe Him for His words' sake, he should believe Him for His works' sake. The kingdom and manifestations of God's power go hand in hand!

The Kingdom Is Breaking Forth With Power
The kingdom of God and the Messiah were intertestamental expectations, and the proof of His kingship was the demonstration of power. Hence, every miracle that took place in the ministry of Jesus was a manifestation of the kingdom. The kingdom manifests whenever you see the works of Satan overturned by the works of Christ. Jesus said that "if I cast out demons by the Spirit of God, surely the kingdom has come upon you" (Matthew 12:28). When the kingdom manifests, the works of Satan in people's lives are reversed; thus, the greatest kingdom manifestation is salvation. At salvation, a person's spirit is made alive again, and he or she is reconciled back to God through belief in Jesus the Messiah. Jesus brought the kingdom in like gangbusters, taking no prisoners and making Satan behave and act right!

The church today is weak for no reason, powerless while having access to power and authority. Consider what Jesus says from the Hebrew Heritage Bible:

> *"...from the days of Yochanan the Immerser until now, the kingdom of heaven is powerfully breaking its way forward, and people breaking out with its power are seizing hold of it."*[15]

> *"The Torah and the Prophets prophesied until John, since then the message of the kingdom is preached, and everyone is forcing his or her way into it."*[16]

Christ is saying in these two texts that the kingdom is being sought with eagerness, with haste, and without fear of consequence. The Greek word that is translated "violent" is the word *biastés* (βιαστής)

---

[15] Matthew 11:12 (Hebrew Heritage Bible).
[16] Luke 16:16 (Hebrew Heritage Bible).

from *bía*, which means "violence, to overpower, impel, but also to rush into." This verb is translated in the Hebrew Heritage Bible in the middle voice, not the passive voice. The middle voice suggests that which someone does for one's self, not another. The Greek word *biazó* (βίαζομαι) for "violence" is taken originally from the Hebrew root *parats* in the Septuagint. *Biazó*, in the middle voice, means "to overpower by force, press hard; to act with violence" for oneself; in contrast, the passive voice means "to be hard-pressed, overpowered." Thus, the use of the noun *biastés* (βιαστής) afterward suggests that people are breaking out with its power and seizing hold of the kingdom. *Harpazó* (άρπάζω) suggests that the people are "seizing" hold of the kingdom! Hence, Jesus is saying that the kingdom was breaking forth, and the people are breaking out with it in a powerful spiritual renewal. The text is interpreted thus: "The kingdom of heaven is powerfully breaking its way forward, and people breaking out with its power are seizing hold of it." Jesus taught that when people hear the message of the kingdom, they embrace the message of the kingdom, and they run into it with passion and break out with its power.

When the text speaks of the "breaking out," it is a reference to Micah 2:13, which provides additional powerful insight. Hence, "breaking out" refers to the same Hebrew term *parats*, which refers to "the breaker." The Midrash states that before the Messiah would come, the breaker would go before Him and prepare the way before Him. In Micah, the word picture is the idea of a shepherd who makes a temporary makeshift fence out of stones in order to provide shelter and protection for their livestock during the night. After the sheep have been confined in the sheepfold during the night, they are anxious to break out. As soon as the breaker, the shepherd, comes and breaks open the gate in the makeshift fence, the sheep break forth, running excitingly in their new freedom. In Micah 2:13, the breaker is Elijah; in the New Testament, the breaker is John the baptizing one (the Elijah of Jewish expectation, Matthew 11:14). Jesus is the shepherd/door in the parable of the lost sheep (Luke

15:4–7) and, as He stated, the "door of the sheep" (John 10:7). Jesus exclaimed that He was the door and that His sheep or kingdom citizens would "enter" by Him and "will go in and out and find pasture" (John 10:9). This is what Jesus states is the case for those who hear the kingdom message or the good news of the availability of the kingdom. The kingdom is both liberating and refreshing! The kingdom of God is God's reign, and His reign is realized when His people receive His power to accomplish His purpose. The church is not a hideout; it is the embassy of the kingdom, where the power of God flows abundantly and people are saved and healed by faith in the King!

Our churches may engage in proclamation and explanation, but where is our demonstration of the gospel of the kingdom? One of the problems with our churches is that we are sociological rather than kingdom-focused, and as a result, we have no ability to demonstrate the power of the kingdom. People need to see the kind of power that points them toward the reality of God and His kingdom so that they will accept our invitation to be born again. Many churches do not flow in demonstration with signs, wonders, and miracles and thus are often ineffective at fulfilling the Great Commission.

Once we turn our focus back to the kingdom of God, we will realize the power that God has given us to walk in supernatural gifts and abilities. Kingdom power overturns all the effects of the fall of man—sickness and disease, unregeneration, chaos, violence, etc. Thus, when we take kingdom authority and heal, prophesy, and witness unto salvation, we have seen the kingdom in action! But the first thing some people do when someone is sick or needs deliverance is call a doctor or psychiatrist instead of turning to God and allowing Him to demonstrate His power. We must understand that although God provides healing through medical science, He is the source of any manifestation of the kingdom, not the medical field.

Jesus and Entering the Kingdom

Jesus preached that the kingdom was at hand, and He inaugurated the kingdom with His incarnation and made it available through His death and resurrection (John 14:6; Galatians 2:20; Colossians 3:1; Romans 8:11, 6:1–11). When Jesus taught about the kingdom, He taught it as an existential reality and a future or eschatological hope. When we speak of the kingdom, we also are speaking of the eternal kingship of God that suddenly broke into time and space in the person of Jesus at a particular place: the land of Israel. So where is the kingdom existentially?

The prevailing discussion in the schools of theology has been the debate over whether or not Christ's kingdom is a part of active history or if it merely pertains to the end times. While emphasizing the end times message of the kingdom as an important aspect of the kingdom of God, C.H. Dodd focused upon its present reality. He is known for his concept of "realized eschatology," which depicted the future power of God manifested in the present ministry of Jesus.

Still others, such as G.E. Ladd in *Inaugurated Eschatology*, attempted to define the kingdom by arguing its presence in the future. He suggested that the kingdom that will come has already begun acting upon the hearts of men and establishing the reign of God until the fullness of the eschatological manifestation. However, regardless of the emphasis used by these scholars, they all agree upon one thing: Each states that the kingdom is here but not in totality—an argument born out in New Testament scriptures:

- Luke 10:9 states: *"And heal the sick there, and say to them, 'The kingdom of God has come near to you.'"*
- Matthew 12:28 reads: *"But if I cast out demons by the Spirit of God, surely the kingdom of God has come upon you."*
- Luke 17:20–21 reads: *"Now when He was asked by the Pharisees when the kingdom of God would come, He answered them and said,*

"The kingdom of God does not come with observation; nor will they say, 'See here!' or 'See there!' For indeed, the kingdom of God is within you."

Thus, the answer to the question "Where is the kingdom of God?" is derived as follows. The kingdom of God is "in our midst." In other words, the kingdom exists around us but cannot be perceived by natural means. Another answer is that the kingdom is wherever the power of darkness is overturned by the power of light—that's the kingdom. As believers, we experience the kingdom of God when the effects of the Adamic nature and its genetic transfer to all humankind are overturned. Thus, the kingdom of God is the realm where the power of God overturns the power of Satan and the results of the fall of man.

Believers are the geography of God. Thus, His kingdom exists anywhere the hearts of men and women have been subjected to His holy will and seek to bring His will to bear in the lives of others. Resident within the placement of God's kingdom is an explanation of its purpose: The ultimate purpose of the kingdom of God is to once and for all overturn and eradicate the effects of the fall of man on humankind, the physical earth, and all living creatures. What is the position of the kingdom of God? It stands in clear opposition to the kingdoms of this world. Satan dominates this age, but God will usher in the "age to come," and He began that process with Jesus' inauguration of the kingdom message.

In Matthew 12:28, Jesus said that the kingdom of God had come upon them—*phthano* [<pha-tha- no> (φθάνω)]: "come on, happen to someone." In Luke 10:9, He told the 70 disciples go and preach the kingdom, cast out demons, heal the sick, operate in the supernatural, and tell the people "The kingdom of God has come near to you"—*eggizo* [<eng-id'-zo> (ἐγγίζω)]: "approach, draw near, be near." Then, in Luke 17:21, Jesus told the Pharisees that the kingdom of God was within them—*entos* [<en-toss> (ἐντός)]: adverb of "place within, inside; among (you), in (your) midst)." From this, we learn that the kingdom of God is near in proximity and experience. It is not just a place of destination; the kingdom of God is approaching and is available now! In the kingdom, we must always deal with the tension of already but not yet: The kingdom is both spiritual and physical, existential and eschatological, an experience and a place. The kingdom is the rule, reign, and realm of God in the hearts of men and women who say yes to the lordship of Christ, but it is also a sphere of existence, the abode of God. Thus, people must be able to experience the kingdom.

How does one enter the kingdom? Jesus teaches us about the prerequisites of the kingdom because the kingdom of God has specific requirements for entry, even for those who claim to know who Jesus is. In John 3:3, Nicodemus came to Christ after seeing Him perform miracles. Nicodemus was a devout Jew and a Pharisee, and like all Jews of that period, He eagerly desired to see the Messiah establish His kingdom on Earth. Christ then informed Nicodemus that unless he was born again, he would never see the kingdom of God. This is an interesting statement because Christ was not talking to a heathen but rather a devout Jew. He was letting him know that he had not received what was necessary to see the kingdom that he so eagerly anticipated. Because of the Jewish people's misguided expectation regarding the kingdom, Nicodemus, along with many other devout Jews, overlooked the obvious signs of the kingdom and thus never saw it. Due to the oppression of the Roman Empire, many Jews of that time expected God's kingdom to overthrow the military presence of Rome, liberate them, and place them in political and military power. Since Christ did not come to inaugurate His kingdom in this manner, they concluded that He could not be the Messiah.

Nicodemus and others who encountered Christ witnessed the many miracles He performed: opening blinded eyes, raising the dead, and cleansing lepers. These miracles were manifestations of the kingdom (Luke 10:9). Christ's performance of miracles provided Nicodemus a glimpse of the kingdom, but Nicodemus was unable to recognize it as such because he had not been spiritually born again. Thus, salvation is the first thing that must transpire before one can see or enter the kingdom. Even though Nicodemus was confused about the kingdom, Jesus did not dismiss his sincere passion for the Messiah and the kingdom but had a conversation with Nicodemus, and understanding that Nicodemus wanted to experience the kingdom of God, He articulated the following:

Jesus answered and said to him, "Most assuredly, I say to you, unless one is born again, he cannot see the kingdom of God."[17]

Jesus answered, "Most assuredly, I say to you, unless one is born of water and the Spirit, he cannot enter the kingdom of God. That which is born of the flesh is flesh, and that which is born of the Spirit is spirit."[18]

Jesus explained for both Nicodemus and us the prerequisite of seeing and entering the kingdom. He discussed the implication of both flesh and spirit. Unfortunately, some have tried to integrate a discussion of water baptism into this text. This text contrasts the difference between the natural birth and the spiritual birth, not water baptism. He refers to the natural birth in terms of water and flesh, and He refers to the spiritual birth in terms of spirit. Jesus was contrasting the difference between a spiritual person and a fleshly person. Then He stated that in order to see and enter the kingdom, one must be born again.

The Greek term used for "born" is *gennaó* (γεννάω), which is a passive voice and means that which someone else does for you. The emphasis is receiving a new origin. The Greek word for "again" is

---

[17] John 3:3 (NKJV).
[18] John 3:5–6 (NKJV).

anothen (ἄνωθεν), which literally means "from above." Thus, this birth is attributed to the Spirit. Jesus informed Nicodemus that the only way to enter the kingdom is through a spiritual rebirth from above. He posits to Nicodemus that the kingdom is an experience by using two strong verbs that highlight the kingdom: "see" and "enter." The two Greek words used in the text are *oida* (οἶδα), which means "to see or perceive, to experience, encounter," and *eiserchomai* (εἰσέρχομαι), which means "go into, enter in." Jesus explained to Nicodemus that the kingdom was not only an experience but was also a place/sphere to be entered into. To enter into the kingdom, one must be born from above. The concept of the new birth is present in the prophetic teachings of Ezekiel in chapter 36:22–33. Thus, when Nicodemus was confused, Jesus stated, "Are you the teacher of Israel, and do not know these things?" (John 3:10). However, the Pharisees at this time were so focused upon the Mishnah (oral traditions of the rabbis) and the Babylonian Talmud (commentary to the Mishnah), along with other Jewish literature, that they lost their focus on the Torah and the prophets. Jesus was clear about entering the kingdom in His teaching and what it required; the concept of the new birth is also present in the Petrine epistle (1 Peter 1:23, 2:2) and in several places in the Pauline epistles. Three common ones are found in 2 Corinthians, Galatians, and Titus (2 Corinthians 5:17, Galatians 6:15, Titus 3:5). This was a concept that was taught as a prerequisite in both the Jewish and Gentile worlds. Jesus was serious when it came to entering the kingdom and the requirements for entry.

What makes someone choose to enter into the kingdom (Matthew 7:21, Isaiah 6:8, Luke 9:23)? It is one thing to see the kingdom and say you are a kingdom citizen; however, it is another thing to enter into the kingdom and actually behave like a kingdom citizen. When the kingdom of God is in us, it is a spiritual reality that shows our reconciliation back to God. When the kingdom is in our hearts, we are reconciled back to God and are connected to Him. Jesus clearly stated that flesh cannot enter the kingdom, which is also an expanded theme throughout the New Testament. Hence, *we* (our fleshly essence) cannot enter the kingdom of God. Therefore, as Luke 9:23 states, *we* must die daily to ourselves, or our flesh. It is the spirit of a person that desires to do the will of God. Only the spirit-man can enter into the kingdom. Sincere worshipers worship in spirit and in truth—they listen to the Holy Spirit for instructions and abide in the Word of Christ as their standard for living (John 4:23–24). Do you really want to enter into the kingdom? Has anyone explained to you the cost of becoming a disciple of Jesus Christ? In a nutshell, the key to entering the kingdom of God is LEAVE YOURSELF BEHIND!

Entering the kingdom (being born again) requires that you function from the DNA of God (2 Peter 1:4). Peter writes that we have been begotten again to a living hope through the resurrection of Jesus from the dead (1 Peter 1:3). Entrance into the kingdom was not made possible until the death and resurrection of Christ; thus, Jesus proclaimed the kingdom in His message and made the kingdom accessible through His crucifixion and resurrection. Jesus further stated in Matthew 18:3 that unless one was converted and became as a little child, they would by no means enter the kingdom. This means that entrance into the kingdom is not the perpetuation of one's natural genetics, which are referred to in the Scriptures as the flesh. Kingdom citizens cannot define themselves by their temperament and personality type; these two are based upon nature and nurture, not the fruit of the Spirit, which is the byproduct of the DNA of the King (Galatians 5:22–23).

I refer to temperaments as Pioneering Paul, People's Peter, Loving Leah, and Exacting Ezra. Hippocrates, the father of medicine, respectively referred to them as the Choleric, Sanguine, Phlegmatic, and Melancholy temperaments. These temperaments are based upon blood flow; they are who you are by your blood type, your Adamic nature, but in order to enter the kingdom, you must have a DNA transfer. Thank God for a kingdom blood transfusion! You must not allow your temperament to rule you if you are going to walk as a kingdom citizen. Kingdom citizens are called to be spiritual and operate out of the fruit of the Spirit, not out of the nastiness of the flesh. The fruit of the Spirit cannot manifest until you die to your flesh, which includes all of the temperaments that we rest in, excuse, and expect others to excuse. It is amazing how many people worship out of their temperaments rather than constantly dying to reveal the fruit of the Spirit. Many Christians will claim salvation through water baptism, yet they have never been reborn in their spirit. Repenting of your sins only to gain intellectual biblical knowledge and not manifest the fruit of a truly reborn nature means you simply brought "yourself" to the water...and dried "yourself" off when you were done!

Christ is looking for sincere worshippers who will worship Him in spirit and in truth (John 4:24). Only your spirit-man can see, hear, and then enter the kingdom! Satan, likewise, is looking for those who nurture their flesh rather than their spirit. Choosing to keep *you*—your flesh, your aspirations, your ambitions, your Adamic nature—is what will keep you out of the kingdom of God! You will be around the things of God, but Satan will use you as his tool.

Have You Chosen to Enter In?
A key indicator that you can use to assess whether you have chosen to enter the kingdom of God is whether you can see the kingdom of God (Isaiah 6, John 3:3). This means can you see with your mind's eye the structure and the principles of the kingdom. Can you see that God desires to dominate your life with His words and that it makes sense to allow Him to do it—can you see it? You cannot enter the kingdom until you see it because the kingdom of God is in the spirit realm, which is only revealed through the vision of who God is, what Christ has done for you, and what God wants to do with your life. This revelation will birth your spirit-man, and you will be able to then see God's vision for your life and fulfill God's purpose in the kingdom. God requires you to see what you're getting into

and how it operates and functions so that you can manifest in your assignment. If God chose to seduce you into the kingdom, He would have violated your free moral agency or taken away your choice. However, God always sets life and death and blessings and curses before you and allows you to choose (Deuteronomy 30:19). As discussed earlier in this session, if you have not seen Christ as King rather than exclusively as your Savior, you cannot see the kingdom of God. Without recognizing the King, you are unable to show reverence, humility, and service to Him and to His appointed officials, who are called to equip you for the work of ministry (Jeremiah 3:15, Ephesians 4:11).

> *"But seek first the kingdom of God and His righteousness, and all these things shall be added to you."*[19]

One must choose to enter the kingdom. And when we give our lives to Christ, we enter God's kingdom and become citizens of the kingdom of God: "You are no longer strangers or foreigners but fellow citizens with saints and members with the household of God" (Ephesians 2:19). Philippians 3:20 states that "our citizenship is in heaven." You are positionally in right standing with God the moment you choose to enter the kingdom. Christ paid the price for your sins, and now you have chosen to live His life (2 Corinthians 5:21). Plainly speaking, it means He is breaking your will and aligning your will with His own. Existentially, we are warring with the flesh every day; hence, we must die to the flesh daily (Luke 9:23). Practically speaking, when you enter the kingdom, God is ruling—He is subjugating.

In order to understand how powerful, present, and preeminent God's kingdom is, we must fully understand the following three unquestionably key aspects about God, His kingdom, and His citizens.

---

[19] Matthew 6:33 (NKJV).

- The Right to Rule
- The Realm of Rule
- The Reality of Rule

1. **The Right to Rule** – The right to rule refers to the authority that has been invested in a king or sovereign to exercise dominion over a kingdom. Only God is vested with the authority and power to rule His kingdom. No other person, power, or being—in the natural or in the spirit—possesses the authority to govern God's kingdom. Right to rule is illustrated in the parable in Luke 19:11–27, when Christ's followers thought His kingdom should appear immediately. When we say that God has the right to rule, we are saying that God and God alone possesses the authoritative power to govern and regulate everything that goes on in His kingdom. No other person, presence, or power carries the privilege or the entitlement to oversee and govern the structure, the operations, or the functioning of anything that occurs in God's kingdom without God's permission. Simply put, He rules.

2. **The Realm of Rule** – The realm of rule refers to the sphere in which ruling authority is exercised. It involves the subjects that are submitted to the one in authority. When you think of a king, you always think of a place. For example, the king of England rules over England. The king of Saudi Arabia is responsible for ruling over Saudi Arabia. The king of Spain rules over the country of Spain. Every king has a domain.

3. **The Reality of Rule** – This aspect focuses upon the actual exercise of royal authority. Even if a sovereign or king has a right to rule and a realm in which he can rule, it is irrelevant if he does not actively exercise his authority. The reality of rule says that not only does God have the authority and power to rule and reign in our hearts and lives, but He actually exercises His right to do so! He actually exercises His authority over the power of Satan.

Thus, God is engaged in His subjects' lives. God is always mandating and controlling—that is what a king does! If God is not ruling where you are, it is not because He is an impotent king. It is probably because you have cut Him and His power off by not acting like a kingdom subject. If you are not acting like a subject, you might very well have lost your citizenship, and you might just be a church member instead of a kingdom citizen!

Romans 14:17 also provides insight on a formal definition of the kingdom of God. Here, the Apostle Paul states that God's kingdom is righteousness, peace, and joy in the Holy Spirit. These three words should define and characterize the life of a person who has confessed Christ as Lord and entered God's kingdom. The Greek word for "righteousness" is *dikaiosuné*, which means "justification or right standing." In Hebrew, righteousness is translated as *tsedeq*, which means "to be right with God or justice." Romans 3 tells us that Jesus became our righteousness and that we were declared righteous through Him! Thus, in order to be in the kingdom of God, one must first be declared righteous based upon the confession of the finished work of Christ. David declared in Psalm 71:15, "My mouth shall tell of Your righteousness and Your salvation all the day, for I do not know their limits." In biblical application, God is righteous and just, Jesus is the Righteous One, and believers become *dikaiosuné* when they repent and allow Christ to become their righteousness.

The Greek word for "peace" is *eirene*, which means "oneness, quietness, rest, or set at one again." The righteous positioning we receive as a result of our confession of Christ as Lord reconciles us into a right relationship with God the Father. Becoming one again with the Father encourages feelings of peace, security, safety, prosperity, and felicity among all kingdom citizens. The Greek word for "joy" is *chara*, which means "cheerfulness, calm delight, or gladness." Joy is the disposition that should characterize the life of all kingdom citizens due to the relationship of peace we enjoy with the Father as a result of being declared righteous by Christ. The kingdom of God is best defined as "the rule of God in the hearts of men who submit themselves to the sovereign will and plan of God for their lives." Having been declared righteous, these men and women now exist in a peaceful relationship with God and experience the joy of a loving relationship with the King. Through forgiveness, we are reconciled and no longer exist in an adversarial relationship with God, so we have peace, which erupts in joy!

Are You Sure You Want to Enter the Kingdom?

If any man desires to come after the King, let him first deny himself (Luke 9:23). You can no longer consult yourself after the King has issued an order. You can't talk to your dead self about the instruction given. When you enter the kingdom, you develop what I call a kingdom mindset. A kingdom mindset or mentality can be characterized by what I have written about in my book, *Introducing the Kingdom*, called the Seven Drivers of the Kingdom and the Four Models of Kingdom ministry. The seven drivers focus upon the following:

- Sovereignty of God
- Structure of God
- Submission to God
- Sonship to God
- Service unto God as a Servant
- Sacrifice unto God
- Stewardship of the Believer

These seven areas drive kingdom behavior, so every kingdom citizen should be aware and sensitive to these Seven Drivers of the Kingdom.

There is a kingdom mindset that must work in tandem with the drivers. I have found four primary focuses that we can find throughout the models of kingdom-minded ministry in both the

Old and the New Testaments. We will examine some practical models that are laced with principles of the kingdom from the Old Testament that expand to the New Testament as we seek to understand the kingdom of God. We must always remember that the Old Testament is the New Testament concealed and the New Testament is the Old Testament revealed. In my examination of the Old Testament, I have discovered four primary models that possess the same kingdom principles and practices; knowledge of these models will assist kingdom citizens and leaders in understanding what effective life in the kingdom of God looks like. The four models are the Mosaic Model, the Joshua Model, the Gideon Model, and the Davidic Model. I will briefly outline the common kingdom principles from the Mosaic Model.

The Mosaic Model

God revealed Himself to Moses as the King who would build a kingdom of priests (Exodus 19:6). Israel understood God as the reigning King (Exodus 15:18), the Most High God (Genesis 14:18–23) who sovereignly reigns over Israel. This kingdom model of ministry highlights some key principles, practices, and pictures that demonstrate kingdom-minded ministry. The four aspects of the kingdom-minded ministry approach are housed and preserved in the Most Holy Place in the Ark of the Covenant beneath the mercy seat in the Tabernacle. The Ark of the Covenant symbolized the covenant between God and man and symbolized that He was Israel's protection because they were under a covenant with God. Housed in the Ark of the Covenant were three things that were considered the "guts" or the essence of the Mosaic ministry:

1. Aaron's rod that budded – God's choice for leadership
2. The Ten Commandments, the Word of God, which detailed the terms of the relationship with the King
3. Manna from heaven, which speaks of the sustainability factors of the kingdom

Thus, the four aspects of kingdom-minded ministry are below:

- **Protection through covenant:** Kingdom citizens understand that they live by the power of a blood covenant that was sealed by the unblemished blood of the Lamb, Christ Jesus.
- **Protocol through leadership:** Kingdom citizens understand the place of spiritual leaders in their lives and honor those whom God has given spiritual rule to. Aaron's rod represents God's choice for leadership. (However, Aaron was not perfect. Remember, Aaron constructed the golden calf, but he was still God's choice.) Respect for spiritual leadership is major in the kingdom.
- **Parameters through the Ten Commandments:** The Decalogue was given in order to establish kingdom boundaries—kingdom dos and don'ts. These parameters were given to regulate both vertical and horizontal relationships. Kingdom people have a high regard for the Word of God, and it controls both their thoughts and actions.
- **Provision through priority:** This implies that the manna from heaven was God's way of letting Israel know that if they were willing and obedient they would eat the good of the land (Isaiah 1:19). Kingdom citizens understand that when they seek the kingdom first, God will provide all their needs!

Beneath the mercy seat, where the blood of the sacrifice and covenant was sprinkled and where forgiveness was rendered to the nation of Israel for an entire year, Aaron's rod, the Ten Commandments, and the manna from heaven were protected. The lesson in this is that God protects the essence of kingdom ministry: protocol, parameters, and provision!

Who Will Not Enter the Kingdom?
While the kingdom is available to all, not everyone will enter it. Let's look at two types of people that the Bible tells us will not gain entrance into His kingdom.

"Not everyone who says to Me, 'Lord, Lord,' shall enter the kingdom of heaven, but he who does the will of My Father in heaven."[20]

1. <u>People whom Jesus does not know</u>

It's interesting that the people denied entrance to the kingdom in this scripture call Christ "Lord," but He stated He never knew them. Jesus is making a tremendous statement: There are people who feel they "know" Him, but He does not know them. How can an all-knowing God not know someone? Jesus was talking about relationship—He knows those who have believed on Him and are born again through His blood. Jesus knows the ones that have denied themselves and serve Him. He stated, "My sheep hear My voice, and I know them, and they follow Me" (John 10:27). The Greek word used for the verb "know" is *ginōskō. Ginōskō* means "to know by personal experience, know intimately." Thus, Jesus intimately knows the people that have a sincere relationship with Him, and it is not characterized by certain religious acts. Thus, religious people know to address Christ as their master and may even flow in the spiritual gifts, but that does not mean God knows them. Jesus was referring to simple churchgoers from the inception of the church, who attend Christian churches out of ritual but don't reflect God's rule and reign in their hearts outside of their Sunday morning services. Christ calls them "practitioners of lawlessness." In their disobedience, they disregard the laws of the kingdom.

As is the case for all governments, the kingdom of God has laws and precepts. Similar to earthly monarchies, the kingdom of God's laws and precepts are established by the Word of the King. Thus, once you have entered into the kingdom, you must govern yourself according to the Bible (the Word of God). The religious group that Christ speaks of in Mathew 7:21 claimed to have done great things for Christ (see verse 22), but they did not adhere to the Word of

---

[20] Matthew 7:21 (NKJV).

God. (The first commandment of God is "Hear, O Israel, the LORD our God, the LORD is one. And you shall love the LORD your God with all your heart, with all your soul, with all your mind, and with all your strength" Mark 12:29–30.) Because of this, they cannot submit to the rule and reign of God. He did call them obedient servants, but He also called them workers of iniquity.

2.   People who serve money
Christ shows us another group of people who will not enter the kingdom in Mark 10:25, which reads, "It is easier for a camel to go through the eye of a needle than for a rich man to enter the kingdom of God." The context of this verse is within the story of Christ's counsel to a wealthy man who desired the eternal life that is received by entering the kingdom. Christ gave this man an invitation of a lifetime and invited this man to follow Him. Think of the scenario—the Incarnate God gives you a personal invitation to discipleship! Wow! Christ had thousands follow Him, yet He extended personal invites to very few outside of the 12. The rich young ruler received the invitation, then Christ informed him that the invitation comes at a cost—everything! Christ made His invitation contingent on this man's ability to value being His disciple above wealth. It was this man's love of money that caused him to reject Christ's kingdom invitation. Christ was not advocating a vow of poverty but was simply making this man decide who was going to have the rule and reign within his heart (Mark 10:17–22).

Jesus teaches us that you cannot serve two masters; you cannot serve God and mammon (money). Loving one means hating the other (Matthew 6:23–25). Money is a form of idolatry to be worshiped and served. While money in and of itself is not a bad thing, the love of money is (1 Timothy 6:10). So if you allow your wealth to rule and reign, you cannot serve money and God too. Notice that Christ didn't attempt to convince the man to rethink his choice; He respected His choice and allowed him to pursue it. Instead, Jesus used the scenario as a teaching moment for His disciples—one from which modern believers can also learn. We have to make the same decision at one time or another in our lives. We have to decide who makes our life decisions for us—God or money (Matthew 6:24). Can you say you would be willing to give up your home, children, spouse, parents, siblings, cars, and all your money if the King required it of you?

Do you want to know when the kingdom of God is in you? When the kingdom is in you, you become radical about your faith. It does not just make you say, "I'm in, and I'm not going to hell!" It causes you to act responsibly about the kingdom. Nothing is subdued, conservative, or laid back in you if the kingdom is in you! If God holds His kingdom message as superior to the message of the kingdom of this world, it must be a radical message! The kingdom is not a religion, it is a movement, and wherever you go, the kingdom is supposed to be radically released!

Seeking the Kingdom Follows Seeing and Entering

We are admonished to seek first the kingdom and His righteousness, and in doing so, God promises to take care of all of our earthly needs (Matthew 6:33). The word "righteousness" is from the Greek term *dikaiosuné*, which literally translates into "right standing." The result of seeing the kingdom is that we want to be right with the King. When we see the kingdom, we desire to enter in and break out with its power, operating in right standing with God! Seeking the kingdom requires that as a kingdom citizen, you stretch toward the kingdom and do what is necessary to accomplish God's will.

Not that I have already attained, or am already perfected; but I press on, that I may lay hold of that for which Christ Jesus has also laid hold of me. Brethren, I do not count myself to have apprehended; but one thing I do, forgetting those things which are behind and reaching forward to those things which are ahead, I press toward the goal for the prize of the upward call of God in Christ Jesus.[21]

With every muscle in you, you have to go after fulfilling your purpose in the kingdom. Many of your secular pursuits will no longer dominate your life. And yes, those not in the kingdom, although they might be in the church, may go by the wayside. No matter what, you must say, "I am going in." You have to stretch. Why? The church mentality will always try to pull you back to its religious traditions and fleshly comfort, while God is saying that you must stretch and seek the kingdom with passion and priority!

Seeking the kingdom not only involves you stretching for the kingdom, but it also involves you speaking the kingdom. The kingdom is based on the Word of God. Kingdom citizens only speak out of two motivations: declare and decree. Decree the orders of the King (Only say what the Father is saying, only do what the Father is doing) and declare the wondrous works of the Lord (John 12:49, Psalm 118:17). When you realize that you are in the kingdom, you are no longer restricted by your flesh, intellect, revenue, and associations. When you understand who the King is and His authority on the earth, your life is simplified to declarations and decrees. You don't speak out of your emotions, sensations, feelings, restrictions, desires, nature, or personality. You only declare formal announcements and decree formal orders, and when the King makes a decree, it must be followed. The Scriptures command us to decree a thing and to declare His praises:

> *"But you are a chosen generation, a royal priesthood, a holy nation, His own special people, that you may proclaim the praises of Him who called you out of darkness into His marvelous light; who once were not a people but are now the people of God…"[22]*

---

[21] Philippians 3:12–14 (NKJV).

[22] 1 Peter 2:9–10a (NKJV).

What words do you find coming out of your mouth? Do you proclaim praises about the King, or do you voice complaints? David stated in Psalm 34:1–2a, "I will bless the LORD at all times; His praise shall continually be in my mouth. My soul will make its boast in the LORD." You must WILL your soul to bless the Lord at all times, to kneel and honor Him at all times, and to fill your mouth with continuous praise. David then said he would never let a life circumstance ever again come and stop him from focusing on who and how God is. He would never get impatient with God and redefine God's goodness in his life. He learned that in losing his mind (1 Samuel 21:10–15), God saved his life when facing death at the hand of the Philistines. Likewise, have you made that decision to lose your mind and take on the mind of Christ (Romans 12:2)? When you are in the kingdom, you understand everything is lovely and getting better every day!

He encourages us not to worry about anything, because He is in control of every aspect of our lives. Thus, seeking first the kingdom involves the following:

- **Perspective** – We often neglect to serve God's kingdom with priority. Christ has died for us, and now we must live for Him. The Apostle Paul states that "I have been crucified with Christ; it is no longer I who live, but Christ lives in me; and the life which I now live in the flesh I live by faith in the Son of God, who loved me and gave Himself for me" (Galatians 2:20). You can enter into the kingdom of God. It is your choice. Choose life or death, blessings or curses. Choose on this day whom you will serve in the spirit! As a part of the kingdom, you are a part of the citizenry of God's kingdom. As a member of the Body of Christ and a co-laborer in ministry, you have tremendous access to the King and the keys to the kingdom. This access is not something that you happen upon nor is it a mystical place into which you stumble. Access into the kingdom is granted to those who first see the spiritual reality of the kingdom and then make the conscious decision to submit to it. Thus, before you enter God's kingdom, you must first be able to see it.

- **Participation/Practices** – All who enter the kingdom have responsibilities to the King. These responsibilities are below:

  o **Worship** – Honor and serve God in lifestyle and focus. Live a life whose aim is to please God according to His Word.

  o **Witness** – Witness to the lost about what you have seen, heard, and experienced with God; share your testimony.

  o **Warfare** – War against the enemy. Shoo away the vultures in your life, and resist the enemy by dousing the fiery darts that come to steal, kill, and destroy your spiritual life.

  o **Wages** – Support the expansion of the kingdom with your income by supporting the local church's efforts through tithes and offerings.

In order to enter the kingdom, you must be able to see it and then seek after it. Thus, kingdom life access is based on revelation (who Christ is) and regeneration (born from above). Entering the kingdom involves surrendering our lives to God Almighty, but there are tremendous benefits to serving God. The kingdom requires focus upon God and God alone, and Christ will reject those who have not made that choice in the end (Mark 8:34–38). Every kingdom citizen must then seek kingdom purpose first. God assures us that when we do, needs will be fulfilled and requests will be granted in His will. Pursue being in the will of God; seek His kingdom and His righteousness (Matthew 6:33).

Chapter Four
Jesus, the Kingdom, and the Cultural Context of Judaism

T HIS BOOK IS ABOUT Jesus' most important parable, the parable of the sower. This parable is the most important parable to know because it must be understood first. Jesus stated in Mark 4:13:

> *"And He said to them, "Do you not understand this parable? How then will you understand all the parables?"*

Thus, it is crucial to first lay a proper foundation for understanding Jesus' most important teaching on the kingdom. Yet, you cannot understand this parable until you understand the King and the historical relevance of the kingdom of God. And we cannot understand the kingdom of God through the lens of colonial rule or British parliament, which do not reflect the Jewish roots of the concept of the kingdom of God. The teachings of Jesus cannot be clearly understood outside of His Jewish context. The meanings of the parables are only unlocked when we recreate the original Jewish context of the parable, as close as we possibly can.

Jesus explained the kingdom from a Jewish perspective; however, the kingdom was not a new concept to the Jewish people. The Jews were very familiar with the theme of the kingdom of God before the words were used during the Intertestamental Period;

the Hebrew Scriptures were laced with it. According to world-renowned Hebrew scholar Dr. Brad Young, while the specific term "kingdom of God" does not appear in the Old Testament except for a single reference to the "kingdom of the LORD," which is found in 1 Chronicles 28:5, the concept of God as King is present throughout the Old Testament. Many allusions are made to "His kingdom." For example, Christ's coming as the King was announced in the Old Testament in the prophetic utterance of Isaiah (9:6–7). The prophet declared that the government would be upon the shoulders of the coming Messiah and that He would sit upon the throne of David. Isaiah goes further by stating that this King would execute justice and judgment and that His kingdom would have no end. In addition, these Old Testament scriptures make very clear references to the King and His kingdom:

- Genesis 49:10 – Refers to the scepter of a king, which symbolizes royal power and authority
- 1 Chronicles 29:11 – Declares that the kingdom and all of creation are the Lord's
- Psalm 103:19 – Declares that the Lord's throne has been established in heaven and that His kingdom rules over all. A throne is the royal seat of a sovereign and represents his reign
- Daniel 4:3 – States that the Lord's kingdom is from everlasting to everlasting

These scriptures clearly refer to the Lord as the King and describe the kingdom over which He shall reign. However, in order to fully understand Israel's perspective of kingdom, we have to reflect on the monarchial rule of King David. In Genesis 12:1–3, God calls Abram: "Now the LORD had said to Abram: 'Get out of your country, from your family and from your father's house, to a land that I will show you. I will make you a great nation; I will bless you and make your name great; and you shall be a blessing. I will bless those who bless you, and I will curse him who curses you; and in you all the families of the earth shall be blessed.'" As a result of His covenant with Abram—whose name was changed to Abraham to represent God's covenant with him—God blesses Abram's grandson, Jacob, with 12 sons. Jacob's name is later changed to Israel, which means "prince," the son of a king. In antiquity, the offspring of these 12 sons became a great nation of people known as the 12 tribes of Israel. God's original people are sometimes referred to as the Israelites, which gives them primary attention as his offspring. "Jews" speaks of the name they were commonly referred to as a new community after the Babylonian exile. We find that after the Babylonian and Persian exile, they were no longer referred to as the northern and southern kingdoms but as Jews. Some writers suggest that the designation of Jews is correlated with Judah and Judea. Thus, the Jews are also the children of Israel. They are sometimes referred to as Hebrews, which refers to their language as a Semitic people. They were a Semitic people with whom God formed a covenant and provided an identity that they did not formerly possess. Today, the descendants of these 12 tribes from 12 sons are commonly known as the Jews and number in the millions. They are God's chosen and covenant people based upon His promises to Abraham.

As it pertained to the first century Jewish nation, the kingdom of God represented a political kingdom. As a result of living under foreign domination for centuries, the Jews lived life expecting God to restore their nation. Dr. Young states that although Israel always saw God as the possessing authority over all the nations of the earth, its existence was characterized by uncertainty, repeated turmoil, and upheaval. As a result, Israel was never able to fully realize and experience the promised blessings of God. Throughout the Old Testament, Israel continually looked toward a more promising future and time when God would act decisively (reign) on her behalf, destroy her enemies, and bring deliverance to His people. Israel was constantly looking for the Messiah—the anointed deliverer who would come to overturn the powers that were controlling her and restore her to new nationalistic and political glory. The Greek word *basileus* [<bas-i-ly-ooce> (βασιλεύς)] means "sovereign, king; denoting the foundation of power." A *basileus* was generally one possessing royal authority. In 1 Samuel 8, Israel demanded that they be given an earthly, natural king to rule over and judge them. God granted their request by appointing Saul as Israel's first *basileus*.

The specialness of the Jewish people, as it relates to them being the historical people of God, has had to undergo many cultural and sociological attacks. The Jewish people are not strangers to persecution and cultural rejection for the sake of the kingdom. Although, as a people, they rejected Christ from a formal theological perspective, to this day, Jews still await *Yeshua Hamashiach*. This is the history, culture, people, theology, and structure into which Jesus was prophesied and made manifest. The Romanization, colonization, and Europeanization of Christianity tried to erase the Jewish roots of Christ. However, it is both a historical and biblical fact that Jesus was a Jew, not a Christian. He did not practice Christianity; He practice Judaism and satisfied the Law. The Bible states that He came to His own, the lost sheep of Israel, and they did not receive Him, but they were still His people (John 1:11–12).

Jesus the Jew

Jesus' pedigree was established through 42 generations (Matthew 1:17). He was born under the Law (Galatians 4:4), He came to fulfill the Law (Matthew 5:17), and when He died, He did so as King of the Jews (Matthew 27:37). While in the last several centuries of Christianity Christ has been portrayed as a European, the Bible clearly depicts Christ as a Jew. This is important because His ethnicity has a great deal to do with the cultural context of His teachings. What is culture? By definition, culture is the "sum total of attitudes, customs, and beliefs that distinguishes one group of people from another." Culture is transmitted through language and other forms of material that depict a way of life. Culture allows us to understand the Scriptures through the lens of the context of Scriptures. The cultural context of Jesus was plain and simple: Jesus was a Jew. The contemporary challenge is that society believes Christ is a European, not Asian, not Jewish. Anti-Semitism, Romanization, and the like re-branded the culture and ethnicity of Christ.

Certain documents are vitally important for gaining some understanding of the cultural context of Jesus with which He Himself was very familiar, such as the Tanakh (the Hebrew Scriptures), Mishnah (oral traditions of the rabbis), Talmud (commentary of the Mishnah), Midrash (teachings of the rabbis on the Torah and the Prophets), and Septuagint (the Greek version of the Hebrew Bible). Judaism was the formalization of the Jewish beliefs and practices that were concretized after the Babylonian exile and defined the cultural context of Christ. The formalization of the law and a strict adherence to it became the antidote for the future threat of exile. The Jews thought that if they could develop and design a code of behavior, they would ensure that they would not violate the Law and the Prophets. This codified behavior was documented in the Mishnah and the Talmud. This behavior and belief system became known as Judaism.

Ezra, who demanded that the Jews put away their strange wives and return to an allegiance to God, is known as the father of Judaism. Ezra demanded that the Jews return back to the Torah and the Prophets before something else dreadful happened to them as a consequence of their unfaithfulness to the covenant of Yahweh. The Midrash, Mishnah, and Talmud became both the protectors of the Law of Moses and that which separated them from the will of God. The practices of Judaism became known as traditions and did not necessary reflect the spirit of the Law. Over time, the essence of the Law got lost in the midst of religious rules and regulations that were designed to protect the Law and the Prophets.

Christ was a product of both His eternal environment and His existential environment, where He was raised subject to Jewish laws and culture. Jesus was raised in this culture as a child; Joseph and Mary practiced these customs, and Jesus adhered to them until He began His Galilean ministry. He was circumcised on the eighth day, according to scripture and customs. He was dedicated and given a Hebrew name at circumcision. Jesus' name in Hebrew is *Yeshua*, which is a shortened form of the word *Yeshoshua*, which in English is "Joshua." Both of the names mean Yahweh is salvation. You will recall that Jesus was named by His Father according to Matthew 1:21; it was the culture for the father to name the child, and thus God, the heavenly Father of Christ, named Him, according to culture.

It is strongly believed that Christ became a bar mitzvah at the age of 12. The bar mitzvah is not a ceremony; it is a status. The term "bar mitzvah" literally means "he who is under (i.e., obligated to do) the Mitzvah, son of the commandments." The next stage of Jewish education was called Beyit-Talmud. Beyit-Talmud means "house of learning." This process in Jewish education was for the boys between the ages of 10 and 14. It was during this time that Jewish boys memorized all of the Tanakh (Joshua through Malachi). This included the writings of the prophets and the Hagiographa. By the time the boys reached the age of 14, they had the whole Tanakh (Old Testament) memorized, or at least knew it very well. Most words in Hebrew include a root (sequence of consonants), and most roots are tri-consonantal or tri-radical (having three consonants). Thus, the word "Tanakh" is built upon the T, N, K: The T is for Torah, the first five books of Moses; the N is for the Nevi'im, the prophetic books; and the K is for Ketuvim for the writings. These are the three major divisions of the Hebrew Bible, which Jesus mastered as a youth. These five years were a very important time of learning for a Jewish boy. It was during this time that they learned the art of rhetorical debating of questions and answers.[23] Thus Luke 2:46 states, "Now so it was that after three days they found Him in the temple, sitting in the midst of the teachers, both listening to them and asking them questions." Jesus was skilled in the Tanakh at a young age. These teachings had been passed down orally by rabbinic teachers in the days of Jesus; other rabbis contributed to the oral Torah until the final recording in 200 AD.

Jesus practiced Jewish culture and participated in the Jewish family systems of behavior. He regularly attended synagogue on the Shabbat. He read the Scriptures at synagogue and expounded upon them. He was recognized as a Jew among both Jews and non-Jews. He attended and participated in the Jewish feasts: Passover, Unleavened Bread, Firstfruits, Pentecost, Day of Atonement or Yom Kippur, Trumpets, and Tabernacles. Many of the narratives of Jesus are identified in time based on the particular feast that was noted. The feasts were a part of the kingdom context of the Jews and were given to them by God the King during the administration of Moses. Jesus began His ministry at the age of 30, which was the time when Hebrew men were believed to have come into full spiritual vigor and the age at which priests were allowed to serve in the temple.

Jesus was unquestionably a Jew, not an African Jew but a covenantal Jew, based upon the Abrahamic and Sinai Covenant. Christ Himself stated that His mission was not to destroy or abolish the Law and the Prophets but to fulfill it (Matthew 5:17), thus Jesus was the fulfillment of the Law and the Prophets. He Himself said on the cross, "It is finished," meaning the demands of the Law had been fulfilled. John, the beloved disciple, wrote in his epistle that Jesus was the propitiation or atonement not simply for the Jews but for the world (1 John 2:2). However, make no mistake,

---

[23] The Online Bible School, "The Jewish Roots of Christianity," Retrieved from http://theonlinebibleschool.net/courses/141-contents-jewish-roots/241-2-jesus-as-rabbi-jewish-roots.html.

worldwide atonement only makes sense through the lens of Jewish culture. The concept of atonement is Jewish. John the baptizing one referred to Jesus as the Lamb of God, who takes away the sins of the world. All of this language means nothing to the Western world or the non-Jewish world because it is a part of the kingdom culture of scripture. Christ the Lamb of God correlates with the tabernacle and the mercy seat, which is symbolic of the throne of God, who dwells in the Holy of Holies. Christ's Jewish culture is germane to really understanding the message of the kingdom. Since Christ was a practicing Jew, He taught the kingdom of God by utilizing the examples of Jewish culture and practices.

Jewish Culture During the Time of Jesus

While I understand it is impractical to expect everyone who reads the Bible to understand Jewish culture in the time of Christ, we must seek to the best of our ability to uncover as much culture as we can in order to understand the message of Christ in context. It is important to note that during the time of Christ, even some Jewish people could not understand His message, even though it was couched in Jewish culture. Thus, understanding Jewish culture alone is not the only key to understanding the message of Christ. We must have the power of the Holy Spirit at work to make all things clear within Jewish culture. When the early church went global to the Gentile world, it had the challenge of explaining divine truths to Gentiles, who existed outside of the Jewish culture. While many Gentiles were exposed to the Jewish culture, especially the more educated class, there were more people in the Gentile world that were unfamiliar with the Jewish culture. But having said this, the early church was extremely effective in its evangelism to the Gentile world and was led by the cross-cultural knowledge of the Apostle Paul. Paul had the challenge of communicating the gospel of the kingdom to the Gentile world by having to reconstruct Jewish culture for them in order for them to embrace Jesus the Messiah. He had the arduous task of taking a local Jesus and making Him global. This entailed having to explain Christ first in culture and then Christ transcending culture. The task of 21st century Christians understanding the Bible while existing in a different culture is not a new quest. However, the contemporary church must understand the rabbi Jesus, who is Jesus the Messiah, and the culture in which He lived.

When Rabbi Jesus came preaching, teaching, and demonstrating the kingdom, He did so as an informal, outside-of-the-establishment teacher. Jesus was referred to as Rabbi Jesus, which was a title of respect in Jesus' culture, not a title that expressed formal ordination of some sort. The term simply meant "great teacher or master." Although He was a bona fide Jew, who was trained in the Law of Moses and Mishnah, He was not a part of nor did He represent the established Jewish faith. The leaders of the establishment were known as Pharisees and Sadducees. The Sadducees originated primarily from the ruling class of priests and aristocrats. Unlike the Pharisees, they did not believe in the resurrection of the dead, and they focused upon the written Torah only as a binding document. The Sadducees were thought to be those who collaborated with the Romans and controlled the worship in the temple. Their influence ceased in 70 AD after the destruction of the temple. Although the Bible does not record their creation, we are introduced to the concepts of the Pharisees, Sadducees, Zealots, Essenes, synagogues, and rabbis in the New Testament. Historically, we know that these groups developed during the Intertestamental Period. Most of those who lived in the land of Judea and Galilee were the descendants of pious Jews who returned to Israel after the Babylonian exile. However, life for them was very uncomfortable due to the pagan ways of the Roman Empire and the heavy taxes levied upon the Jews. It is no surprise that all Jewish people anticipated a day of liberation and emancipation from the harsh treatment of their Gentile oppressors. The social and political times and conditions of the Jews during the time of Jesus demanded a manumission and a Messiah. Thus, during the time of Jesus, political intensity and spiritual fervor were both escalating.

Oftentimes in the New Testament, you will read about the synagogue, which was an important part of Jewish culture and Jesus' life. Synagogues are thought to have possibly developed during the Babylonian exile in the sixth century BC, when the Jews were unable to worship in the temple in Jerusalem. The local synagogue served as a community center where people gathered to pray and study the Scriptures. The synagogues served multiple purposes in antiquity; during the week, it served as school, and on the Sabbath, it served as a gathering place for prayer and studying the Scriptures.

The culture of Jesus was an agrarian, farming culture; it was a culture that was also filled with entrepreneurship because everyone had a particular skill, and through their craft, they made their living. Jesus used Jewish culture to explain the message of the kingdom. Thus, parables, which where natural illustrations that were used to explain the spiritual character and content of the kingdom of God, were the vehicles in which He taught His kingdom principles. Jesus' primary purpose for utilizing parables was to exhort the people to live godly and moral lives by being in a right relationship with God and others based upon the Scriptures. Oftentimes Jesus would find Himself in a situation where He was posed with a question, some sincere and some insincere. He would teach and oftentimes conclude His teaching with a couple of parables.

Christ's kingdom teachings were carried out through the use of parables. This rabbinic, parabolic approach to teaching was a fascinating approach. Dr. Brad Young, in his books, *Jesus the Jewish Theologian* and *Jesus and the Jewish Parables*, describes that parables were one-act, live dramas with a specific function. Parables served as teaching aids that principally underscored a central point. Jesus, as a Jewish rabbi, practiced the rabbinic tradition of parables, as was the custom of rabbis. The rabbis utilized parables in order to communicate the teaching of the Mishnah. The Mishnah was divided into six sections that were used to govern the culture and practice of Jewish life to ensure that they were adhering to the Law of Moses and the Prophets, but of course, Jesus alerted them to the fact that they were more committed to their traditions than the Word of God (Matthew 15:3–9).

The Mishnah taught through its Six Tractates:

1. Order of Seeds
2. Festivals
3. Women
4. Damages
5. Holies (temple and sacrifices)
6. Purities

The Mishnah was and still is today a very important document in Judaism as it relates how the practice of Judaism is to be carried out. Jesus was trained and schooled in the Mishnah and the Talmud, its commentary. Thus, Christ had to maneuver around the traditions of the rabbis in order to communicate the Word of God. We must understand the cultural context of Christ's teachings if we are going to truly grasp the meaning of Christ's teachings.

Jesus' culture was a Jewish culture filled with rabbis who were trained in the Scriptures and were considered wise and masterful teachers who traveled from village to village, dropping knowledge of the Scriptures. In order to ensure that the rabbi's teachings were sound, the Pharisees and other religious leaders would listen in on the teachings and either validate or invalidate their teachings. Jesus the Messiah was quite the phenomenon, such a wise rabbi, yet hailing from Nazareth, which was the equivalent to the inner cities of America, the ghettos of Africa, or the poor communities worldwide. Jesus was not born with a silver spoon but with a divine vision. And the question that emerged among the people was "Can anything good come out of Nazareth?" Jesus was not from the suburbs; He was from the hood, skilled in Judaism but wise in game and street deception. He was well prepared for the trick questions of the aristocratic religious leaders of His day, who constantly attempted to trap Him in His teachings.

Rabbi Jesus taught utilizing the rabbinic traditions of proclamation, explanation, and demonstration. Using this methodology, Christ made the message of the kingdom of God and its existence plain to the disciples. He also took the traditional rabbinic approach of arguing from minor to major points, for which rabbis were known. Jesus would always make "koshers" or connections between His teachings and the Hebrew Scriptures. Jesus the Messiah's (*Yeshua Hamashiach*) concentration or main theme in teaching was the kingdom of God/kingdom of heaven. This is the theme with which He began His public ministry, and the kingdom of God was the last topic of discussion Jesus had with His disciples before His ascension (Acts 1:3). The kingdom of God was the principal cause for which Jesus lived and died; it is the kingdom that He explained in His teachings, it was the kingdom that He illustrated in His parables, and it was the kingdom in which He demonstrated miracles, signs, and wonders.

Chapter Five
He Spoke All Things in Parables

T HE TITLE OF THIS book is *Welcome to the Kingdom,* and while I have provided you with much needed information about the kingdom, the second half of this book will move us into the direct discussion of the parable of the sower. I want to introduce you to the world of the kingdom based upon the teachings of Jesus in the parable of the sower, seed, Satan, and the soil, but let's first discuss parables in general.

Parables were the chief means of teaching the gospel of the kingdom. What is a parable, and what makes them so effective? Parables were a teaching and literary form used in both the Old and the New Testaments. However, the most famous teacher who used parables was the great Jewish rabbi, Jesus. In these parables, He explained the kingdom of God and proclaimed its gospel message. Jesus was an amazing storyteller, who was skilled in communicating His message. Parables were paramount to communicating the message of the kingdom. Jesus did not teach His disciples without utilizing parables: "But without a parable He did not speak to them" (Mark 4:34).

The Telling of the Tale
The Lion and the Mouse, The Tortoise and the Hare, The Fox and the Grapes, and *The Boy Who Cried Wolf* are just a few of the stories attributed to the legendary Greek fabulist, Aesop. Believed to be

an Ethiopian slave born in the region of Thrace, Phrygia, otherwise known as Athens, Aesop is believed to have lived from 620 to 560 BC. Despite his status, Aesop appears to have worked as a kind of personal secretary to his master and to have enjoyed a great deal of freedom. His reputation was derived from his skill at telling fables as illustrations of points in an argument, even possibly in court.[24] During his lifetime, he is believed to have written more than 150 fables. The word "fable" comes from the Latin word *fabula*, which means "story," and is derived from two Latin root words: *fari*, which means "to speak" and -*ula*, which means "little." Thus, fables are properly defined as "little stories." Today, fables are largely regarded as children's tales. However, in ancient Greece, they were used to illustrate moral truths and maxims. Written in prose or verse, plants, animals, mythical creatures, inanimate objects, and forces of nature take on human qualities in order to express the truth, or the storyteller's opinion, in an inoffensive manner that can be easily understood by everyone. This literary device is called anthropomorphism.

Aesop was so talented at creating the moral vignettes that most memorable vignettes have become attached to his name, regardless of their date of origin or authorship. Following his death, Aesop's fables were revised and translated into other languages numerous times by numerous people around the world. As a result of the addition of material from other cultures and changes in the meanings of words based upon translations, the body of work known and referred to as *Aesop's Fables* has become an integral part of the heritage of Western literature and folklore. While Aesop's fables are certainly engaging and communicate well-established axioms or subjective moral truths, they are by no means unique. In fact, fables, allegories, and short stories have been used throughout the ages to communicate truths and opinions that would ordinarily

---

[24] Enotes.com, "Aesop Biography," Retrieved from http://www.enotes.com/topics/aesop.

be derogatory in nature in a much more palatable manner. Such was also the case with Christ and His use of parables to disseminate the message of the kingdom of God.

Which would you say that you are more familiar with: Aesop's fables or the parables in the Bible?[25]

Fables are:	Knowingly untrue, unrealistic fantasy stories that illustrate previously discovered human wisdom.	**But parables are:**	True or realistic stories that illustrate a deep spiritual truth not previously understood by man.
Myths are:	Fantasy/untrue stories that are accepted as reality/truth.	**But parables are:**	Stories that clearly delineate the story part and the spiritual lesson being taught.
Proverbs are:	Short sayings to be taken literally to teach some obvious human wisdom.	**But parables are:**	Longer and more illustrative and teach a hidden truth.
Allegories:	Transfer the properties of one thing to another.	**But parables are:**	Stories that compare two separate things to one another.

---

[25] Bible.ca, "The Parables of Jesus: Overview and Summary," Retrieved from http://www.bible.ca/d-parables-of-jesus.htm

A survey of the gospels shows Jesus teaching many things to the disciples using parables. The word "parable" comes from the Greek word *parabolé* (par-ab-ol-ay'), which means "comparison." *Parabolé* is a derived compound word from *paraballo*: *para*, meaning "from, of, at, by, besides, or near," and *balló*, meaning "to throw or to let go of a thing." Thus, *parabolé* means "to put one thing by the side of another for the sake of comparison." Within the New Testament Scriptures, Christ used parables to place a truth alongside something that was known and familiar. Thus, parables are not simply metaphors. Rather, they are "alongside teachings," stories that use something that is familiar, within which is housed the truth of what is being taught, in order to communicate a deeper message.

Outside of the gospels, the word *parabolé* only appears in the New Testament in the book of Hebrews. Hebrews 9:8–9 reads as follows:

> *...the Holy Spirit indicating this, that the way into the Holiest of All was not yet made manifest while the first tabernacle was still standing. It was symbolic for the present time in which both gifts and sacrifices are offered which cannot make him who performed the service perfect in regard to the conscience—*

Referring to the tabernacle in verse 8, the author of Hebrews states that the tabernacle and the sacrifices offered there were symbolic— the word "symbolic" being translated as *parabolé*. Additionally, Hebrews 11:19 (ESV) states that Abraham, "figuratively speaking," received Isaac back from death after proving he was willing to sacrifice his son. Here, the phrase "figuratively speaking" is also translated as *parabolé*. The word *parabolé* was the word used only by the synoptic writers: Matthew, Mark, and Luke. It is translated from the Hebrew word *mashal* in the Septuagint 28 out of 39 times. *Mashal* (<maw- shawl' >, (מָשָׁל)) means "proverb, parable, proverbial saying, aphorism, byword, similitude, parable, or sentences of ethical wisdom, ethical maxims."

Christ, Parables, and the Gospels

An examination of the gospels will reveal that one-third of Christ's teachings were delivered in the form of parables. As such, Christ's method of teaching did not resemble the method and/or technique of any of His contemporaries. Regarding His teaching style, the scriptures indicate the following:

> *"And so it was, when Jesus had ended these sayings, that the people were astonished at His teaching, for He taught them as one having authority, and not as the scribes."*[26]

At the end of the Sermon on the Mount, people marveled at His teachings. Not only was Christ's message of the kingdom of God new to the people listening but His delivery to the hearing public was also novel. The significance of these two facts is found in the Scriptures:

> *"All these things Jesus spoke to the multitude in parables; and without a parable He did not speak to them, that it might be fulfilled which was spoken by the prophet, saying: "I will open My mouth in parables; I will utter things kept secret from the foundation of the world."*[27]

Christ's use of parables as His primary means of teaching was a fulfillment of Old Testament prophecy.

The parables taught by Christ can be generally categorized as one of four primary types:

1. **Nature Parables:** These parables juxtapose the two realities of God's kingdom, indicating its beginning to be imperceptibly small but eventually becoming an all-encompassing reality. Examples of these parables include the following:

---

[26] Matthew 7:28–29 (NKJV).
[27] Matthew 13:34–35 (NKJV).

- The Mustard Seed (Mark 4:30–32)
- The Growing Seed (Mark 4:26–29)
- The Leaven (Matthew 13:33)

2. **Discovery Parables:** These parables show the value of possessing God's kingdom and indicate that it should be desired as a possession above and beyond other natural possessions. Its discovery causes the wise to abandon all in order to obtain it. Discovery parables include the following:
   - The Hidden Treasure (Matthew 13:44)
   - The Pearl of Great Price (Matthew 13:45–46)
   - The Great Dragnet (Matthew 13:47–50)

3. **Contrast Parables:** Among other things, these parables compare examples of negative attitudes or actions related to God's kingdom with positive attitudes or actions related to God's kingdom. Contrast parables include the following:
   - The Pharisee and the Tax Collector (Luke 18:9–14)
   - The Lost Sheep, the Lost Coin, and the Lost Son (Luke 15:4–32)

4. **Fortiori Parables:** These parables depict the logic of "How much more?" or "from lesser to greater." They are based upon the following line of reason: If sinful man would not act in a certain evil or foolish way or, conversely, if man is capable of demonstrating certain attributes, how much more can God be depended on to behave righteously and be beneficent? This is demonstrated throughout the Scriptures by Christ repeatedly asking, "How much more will your Father in heaven give?" (Luke 11:13).

According to Bible scholars and theologians, early rabbis' writings included parables. Their parables began or ended with, as well as explained, Old Testament texts. Yet Jesus' use of parables differed from that of Old Testament teachers. These scholars also indicate that Jesus came not to exegete scripture but to reveal the new dispensation of the kingdom of God. Not all parables taught by Christ, however, are categorized as strictly kingdom parables. As opposed to revealing the reality of the kingdom, some parables are more general and simply illustrate a kingdom principle. To be precise, kingdom principles normally begin with Christ declaring, "The kingdom of God is like..." and continuing with the description of a word picture that is used to increase the understanding of the hearers. However, the remainder of Christ's parables—those that do not begin with these words and are simply referred to as the parables of Jesus—are still very relevant to the life of the believer. The lessons contained in them are valuable in and of themselves.

Parables in the Synoptic Gospels			
	Matthew	Mark	Luke
Lamp under a Basket	5:14–15	4:21–22	8:16–17, 11:33
Wise and Foolish Builders	7:24–27		6:47–49
New Cloth on an Old Garment	9:16	2:21	5:36
New Wine in Old Wineskins	9:17	2:22	5:37–38
The Sower	13:3–8	4:3–8	
Wheat and Tares (Weeds)	13:24–30		8:5–8
Mustard Seed	13:31–32	4:30–32	13:18–19
Leaven (Yeast)	13:33		13:20–21
Hidden Treasure	13:44		
Pearl of Great Price	13:45–46		
Fish in the Net	13:47–50		
Lost Sheep	18:12–14		15:4–7
Unmerciful Servant	18:23–35		
Workers in the Vineyard	20:1–16		
Two Sons	21:28–32		
Wicked Tenants (Absent Landlord)	21:33–41	12:1–9	20:9–19
The Wedding Banquet	22:2–14		

Fig Tree	24:32-35	13:28–31	21:29–33
The Thief in the Night	24:36-44		
Absent Householder		13:32–37	
Ten Virgins	25:1–13		

Parables in the Synoptic Gospels			
	Matthew	**Mark**	**Luke**
Talents (Matthew); Minas (Luke)	25:14–30		19:11–27
Growing Seed		4:26–29	
Moneylender and Two Debtors			7:41–43
Good Samaritan			10:30–37
Friend at Midnight			11:5–8
Rich Fool			12:16–21
Watchful Servants			12:35–40
Faithful Servant			12:42–48
Barren Fig Tree			13:6–9
Great Banquet			14:16–24
Counting the Cost			14:28–33
Lost Coin			15:8–10
Lost Son			15:11–32
Shrewd Manager			16:1–9
Unworthy Servants			17:7–10
Persistent Widow			18:1–8
Pharisee and the Tax Collector			18:9–14

Wise Sayings of Christ in John

The word *parabolé* (parable) does not appear in the gospel of John. However, in John 10:6 and John 16:25, 29, the word for "illustration, figure of speech, allegory" is used, which is the Greek word *paroimia* (par-oy-mee'-ah), which means "wise saying" or "riddle." Thus, the stories commonly referred to as parables found within the gospel of John include the following:

Wise Sayings	Reference
Blowing Wind	3:8
Bridegroom's Attendant	3:29
Fields Ripe for Harvest	4:35–38
Father and Son	5:19–20
The Slave and the Son	8:35
Good Shepherd	10:1–5
Twelve Hours of Daylight	11:9–10
Kernel of Wheat	12:24
Walking in the Light	12:35
Preparing a Place	14:2–4
The Vine and the Branches	15:1–8
Woman in Travail	16:20–24

Although usually referred to as parables, none of these stories are presented in the same form as the longer true parables found in Matthew, Mark, and Luke. However, Jesus' unique style of teaching is still apparent within each of these short descriptors, helping to establish a sense of continuity between John's gospel and the synoptic gospels.

It can be somewhat difficult to discern what type of literary form is being used in the Bible without spiritual instruction. Some stories, on face value, look like parables but are not. The following passages look like parables but are not. Luke 14 contains two stories/sayings that give instructions on conduct: "Take the lowly place" in verses 7–11 and "feast for the poor" in verses 12–14. Then, in Matthew 25:31–46, the story of sheep and goats foretells of future events but is not a parable. The story about the rich man and Lazarus (Luke 16:19–31) does the same thing.

Christ, the Kingdom Message, and Parables

The wise kingdom sayings of Christ in the gospel of John are above. Each parable conveys a specific kingdom principle that helps reveal and explain aspects of the kingdom. Although mentioned earlier, the parables that Christ taught specifically on the kingdom of God in the synoptic gospels are:

1. The Sower (Matthew 13:3-8, Mark 4:3-8, Luke 8:5-8)
2. The Wheat and the Tares (Matthew 13:24-30)
3. The Mustard Seed (Matthew 13:31-32, Mark 4:30-32, Luke 13:18-19)
4. The Leaven (Matthew 13:33, Luke 13:20-21)
5. The Hidden Treasure (Matthew 13:44)
6. The Valuable Pearl (Matthew 13:45-46)
7. The Great Dragnet (Matthew 13:47-50)
8. The Owner of a House (Matthew 13:52)
9. The Unmerciful Servant (Matthew 18:23-34)

Approximately one-third of Christ's recorded teachings are in the form of parables. What do they mean? These lessons are the core of Christ's teachings and provide startling revelations regarding God's kingdom.

Interpreting Parables

Parables generally possess the following characteristics:

- Clear, concise, simple in detail, and easily understood by everyone
- Speak of familiar experiences, those of everyday life
- Kingdom-centered and direct people to the kingdom of God
- Ending is significant and is often surprising, a reversal of what is expected
- Usually has a single, main point that Jesus wants to drive home, often found in the ending

Although this list of characteristics might lead one to believe that properly interpreting the parables of Christ is an easily accomplished feat, the opposite is actually true. Christ taught using parables, not as a method of entertainment but as a means of rousing His listeners' thinking. As such, parables did not encourage passive listening. Instead, they demanded close attention, examination, and requisite, corresponding action. Additionally, the parables served to obscure the truth of the lesson being taught from those who refused to respond.

Consider the parable of the sower, found in Matthew 13, Mark 4, and Luke 8. At the conclusion of His teaching, Christ states, "To you it has been given to know the mystery of the kingdom of God; but to those who are outside, all things come in parables, so that 'Seeing they may see and not perceive, and hearing they may hear and not understand; lest they should turn, and their sins be forgiven them'" (Mark 4:11b–12).

This is followed by Christ's explanation of the parable of the sower to the disciples. He tells them explicitly that they have been granted special access to not just the kingdom of God, which in and of itself is a mystery to men, but also to the mysteries of the kingdom of God. The Greek word for "mystery" is *mustérion* (moos-tay'-ree-on), which is defined as "a hidden thing, secret, or mystery that is confided only to the initiated." Thus, Christ is stating that they have been given access to a mystery within a mystery—something to which the world had not yet had access.

No one will argue the power and effectiveness of Christ's parables in communicating the kingdom message. His technique, imagery, and use of easily understood, everyday events and experiences, which were common to the people of Palestine, were masterful. In the past, many interpreters allegorized the parables, looking for symbolic significance in as many details of the stories as possible.

For example, St. Augustine (354–430 AD) explained the parable of the good Samaritan (Luke 10:30–37) in the following way:

- The man going down from Jerusalem represented Adam leaving the peaceful place that was Eden.
- The robbers who beat him were the devil and his demons, who persuaded Adam to sin.
- The priest and the Levite (the Law and the Prophets) offered the victim no help, but the Samaritan (Christ) rescued him, pouring oil and wine (comfort and exhortation) onto the man's wounds.
- The donkey on which the Samaritan (Christ) placed the man symbolized the church. The innkeeper was represented by the Apostle Paul.

By contrast, many modern interpreters have abandoned the allegorical approach; they believe that each parable has only one main point. Others argue that a parable might make as many as three main points: one for each of the main characters in the story.

Modern scholars employ and encourage others to utilize the following tips when interpreting parables:

1	Note the "rule of end stress:" The climax and point of most parables comes at the end.
2	Identify the principles that are present that reveal the character of God, aspects of His kingdom, how He wants to relate to humanity, and how He expects humankind to respond to Him.
3	Ask what the parable indicates about one's relationship with God and Christ.

4	Ask what the parable indicates is expected of kingdom citizens.
5	Identify what the parable indicates should be one's general attitude about and toward the kingdom of God.

Recognize that not every detail of a parable is meaningful unless the context demands it. Additionally, don't rely on static symbolism, thinking that symbols mean the same thing in each and every parable where they are used. For example, in the parable of the sower, the seed represents the Word of God, and the soil represents the human heart. However, in the parable of the wheat and the tares, the good seed represents the children of the kingdom, and the field represents the world.[28]

Since parables are a teaching device used by Jesus, a Jewish rabbi, it is of utmost importance to select someone trained in exegesis and not eisegesis. Parables make it clear that one must have a well-trained scholar of the Word to do the necessary research and study to interpret exactly what the text is saying. Parables use first century Palestinian cultural references to make a point, and these points can be lost on the 21st century Western-influenced reader.

Christ's use of parables as His primary means of teaching was both prophetic and purposeful. Parables were used to communicate the hidden mysteries of the kingdom of God to Christ's inner circle of disciples as well as teach the masses general kingdom principles and expectations.

---

[28] Answers.libertybaptistchurch.com, "The Parables of Jesus Christ," Retrieved from http://answers.libertybaptistchurch.org.au/answers/14.pdf.

Parables were the preaching illustrations of Jesus that were designed to assist the listener to grasp the point of the teaching. Parables appealed to the listening audience on multiple levels, appealing to the common and intellectual listener. The parable conveys a deeper dimension of truth than the literal story, and not every aspect of the story is to be thought of allegorically. Jesus' teachings were always designed to communicate a theocentric message of the kingdom. Understanding Jewish culture and parables is the foundation for understanding the message of the kingdom.

Chapter Six

The Parable of Preeminence

K INGDOM PARABLES ARE SPIRITUAL truths that aid the listener in understanding what the kingdom is and how it operates. God wants us to understand the kingdom; it is not acceptable to say, "I don't understand the Bible; it's so confusing," and then just give up! A primary way that God helps us to understand the kingdom is through the truths told by Jesus in the parables.

The ministry and message of Christ are inundated with the concept of the kingdom of God. This makes sense because He came to Earth, the King's domain, to teach us about God. References to the King's kingdom are prevalent throughout the New Testament:

- Matthew and Luke recount that Jesus was born a king (Matthew 2:2, Luke 2:11).
- John the Baptist preaches the message "Repent for the kingdom of heaven is ready. Are you?" (Matthew 3:1–2).
- Jesus comes after John and preaches and teaches the kingdom of God (Matthew 4:17).
- Jesus commissioned 12 disciples to preach, teach, and demonstrate the kingdom of God (Matthew 10:5–7).
- Jesus later commissioned an additional 70 men to preach the kingdom (Luke 10:1–12).

- Acts 1 opens with the disciples asking if Jesus will restore the kingdom back to Israel at that time (v. 6).
- The last chapter of the book of Acts shows us Paul in a rented house, teaching the things of the kingdom (28:30–31).
- Romans 14:17 defines the kingdom, telling us that the kingdom of God is not meat and drink but righteousness, peace, and joy in the Holy Ghost. It is not about self-consumption and personal prosperity.
- Revelation shows us the concept of the kingdom reaching a significant apex when Jesus returns as King to war for Israel at the Battle of Armageddon (Revelation 16:16).
- Revelation also foretells of the total fulfillment of the kingdom of God when Satan, Death, Hades, and anyone not found written in the Book of Life are eternally cast into the lake of fire and He establishes a new heaven and a new earth (20:11–15).

The Parable of Preeminence

Jesus taught the disciples about the kingdom of God on multiple occasions. After Jesus' teachings to the disciples, commonly known as the "Sermon on the Mount," and various miracles, the disciples had already been told to preach, teach, and demonstrate the kingdom of God. They had already been given kingdom power to cast out unclean spirits and heal all kinds of diseases and sicknesses (Matthew 10:1, Mark 3:13–15). According to Mark 4:2, Jesus taught the disciples and the multitudes many things in parables. However, the parable that was recorded for mankind in all three synoptic gospels is the parable of the sower (Mark 4:1–20, Matthew 13:1–23, and Luke 8:4–15).

On the day of this teaching, Jesus, in a boat on the sea, taught both the 12 and the multitude. However, later, when He was alone, Jesus explained the parable to the 12 and "those around Him" (possibly some of the 70 disciples – Mark 4:10) when asked. The parable used terms and imagery that would be easily understood by the people of that time: sowers, seeds, soils, and birds. While the natural importance of these elements was readily identifiable to believers in the first century, their spiritual significance was less discernible. Even the disciples did not understand the parable Jesus taught; that is why they asked Him questions privately for a greater understanding. Christ used this private moment to expound on the relationships that exist between the natural elements of the parable and their spiritual counterparts. As such, any study of kingdom parables must begin here. Jesus Himself asked, *"Do you not understand this parable? How then will you understand all the parables?"* (Mark 4:13). Therefore, it is clear that God expects us to understand this parable first.

Since Jesus clearly tells us that we must understand this parable before all other parables, I refer to this parable as the parable of preeminence.

By now, you may be wondering why Christ was so emphatic about this parable being studied and understood first. The answer, of course, has to do with the message of the kingdom—this is the parable upon which the kingdom message is largely built in the New Testament. Possessing a limited or skewed understanding of this parable or, worse yet, not understanding this parable at all, will result in everything else you learn about the kingdom of God being completely off. Understanding the parable of preeminence is critical in order for you to live out your life as a kingdom citizen. It outlines four of the most critical variables in your kingdom walk:

The Sower	The sower has two spiritual representations for us. First, the sower represents Christ. He is the Word of God who also sows the Word of God. Secondly, the sower is our fivefold ministry gifts, whom Jesus has given authority to sow the Word of God into our lives (Ephesians 4:11–12).
The Seed	The seed represents the Word of God that is sown. It is the life-giving Word that houses the will of God, gives us faith, equips us for ministry, and renews the mind, and it is one of the most effective weapons we have against the enemy.
The Soil (or ground)	The soil represents the four possible conditions of the human heart when the Word is sown. Any time the Word is sown, you can be any one of these types of soil. The parable clearly tells you what will happen with each type of soil.
The Bird	The bird represents the enemy, who comes for the Word's sake. Any time the seed is sown into the soil of your heart by the sower, Satan is standing close by to steal the Word so that it does not bear fruit or bring a return in your life.

Sower/Seed

The words "sower" and "seed" are derived from the same Greek word, *speiró. Speiró* [<spi'-ro>, (σπείρω)] means "to sow" and "sower or farmer." Saying that the sower sows implies that he is sowing seed; thus, the word "seed" does not appear in this passage.

The Four Soil/Ground Types

After providing a definition regarding the spiritual meaning of each of the elements in the parable of the sower, Christ offered the following explanation of what happens in the kingdom of God with regard to the sower, the seed, the soil, and Satan. The preacher preaches the Word. As he preaches, there are potentially four types of individuals who will hear and respond to the Word. The parable gives insight into how they will respond, both then and even now.

Wayside Ground

This type of ground is the ground that the sower walked upon while he scattered the seed into the tilled soil; it was on the "side of the way" where he would trod. When he reached into his bag and pulled his hand out, some of the seed inadvertently fell onto this hard-packed, solid ground. Since no seeds could penetrate this type of ground, nothing could ever grow there. This type of ground represents people who come to worship so preoccupied with their own issues that they never truly hear a message at all. While the sower is sowing the Word, none of the precious seed ever has a chance to penetrate them.

Like the hard-packed, trodden-down, wayside ground, they are tightly self-consumed and beaten down with the issues of their own lives. Further, because the seed of the Word never penetrates the soil of their hearts, they never experience the life-changing transformation it can bring. Instead, the seed sits on the surface of their wayside soil, just waiting for Satan to come and eat it as the birds ate the seeds off of the hard, wayside ground in the field. For these people, just as quickly as the Word comes, it is taken away. In the English language, "wayside" is translated as *hodos*. *Hodos* [<hod-os'>, (ὁδός)] means "road, by implication, a route or path." The farmers walked on the pathways between the tilled soil until it became packed down and formed a pathway. Thus, the wayside ground could not produce because it was not tilled and made ready to receive the seed.

Stony Ground

This type of ground is that soil which has a thin top layer and then stone underneath. It looks like good, penetrable ground; however, the layer of stone underneath only allows shallow growth because the roots are not able to grow deep below the surface to reach life-sustaining water. Thus, as soon as the heat of the sun hits the small plant, it scorches it. The short-lived plant withers up and dies. The stony ground heart represents the heart of the person who gets excited about serving God during a service but is not committed to a life in total submission to Him.

These are the people who come to have a good time at church, enjoying the music and the people, and they are even committed, at the time, to live for God. However, they do not commit to study of the Word or learn how to live for God according to His wisdom to create the deep reservoir of internal fortitude needed in times of trouble. Thus, as soon as they experience the challenges and pressures of life, they turn back to what they know: carnal lives that are lived for Satan rather than God. Their excitement for God is palpable but short-lived because their roots are shallow. With their mindset, it is impossible for them to have a lasting relationship with God. Stony ground was characterized by two aspects: its lack of depth and the rocks contained within it. Similar to the relationship between the words "sower" and "seed," the word "ground" does not appear in the Greek text. "Stony" in the Greek is *petródés* [<pet-ro'-dace>, (πετρώδης)], which means "rock-like or rocky." *Petródés* is a compound word: *petra* meaning "little rock" and *eidos* meaning "appearance or shape."

Thorny Ground

This type of ground represents ground that allows for good growth, but it is contaminated with weeds. Thus, when a plant grows nice and strong, with deep enough roots to sustain it long term, the weeds that surround it grow up around the plant and choke the life out of it over time. While it appears that the plant will have a long, healthy life (Luke records that it grows fruit, but not to maturity), weeds are allowed to get too close, its life is cut short, and it dies. This soil is representative of people who have been seriously and sincerely engaged in the things of God for some time. However, because they did not watch their associations, hanging around carnal people who did not have a heart for God, the cares of this world, the deceitfulness of riches, and the desire for other things choked the Word out of them. Once spiritually vibrant, they now appear spiritually dead—almost as if they never had a walk with Christ at all. They no longer seem like the same people, because they are not—all of the Word has been choked out of them. Caution: If you consider church to be "in the way" of anything you are trying to accomplish in life, you may be thorny ground!

Good Ground

This type of ground is useful, healthy soil that is conducive for long-term, safe, and sustainable growth. It represents the hearts of people who hear the Word, accept the Word, and allow the Word to work in their lives according to its design. Thus, they grow and produce at levels that are thirty-fold, sixty-fold, and a hundred-fold. These people are productive for the King! This soil represents people who not only receive the Word sown in their lives but also apply its wisdom to their lives. They are not just hearers of the Word but doers; they are constantly engaged in soil maintenance. Just as they receive the Word, they are equally guarded against non-scriptural thoughts and teachings, carnal people, and sinful environments. This soil represents humble people who put no confidence in their own flesh but in God alone, trusting in His Word to complete them. Thus, this soil endures to the end. When Jesus used the word "good" to describe the last soil that was productive, He used *kalos*. *Kalos* [<kal-os'>, (καλός)], by translation, means "good, beautiful." The word "good," as used in this verse, implies value or virtue in its ability to be used and thus is distinguished from *agathos*, which means "intrinsic goodness."

The Interactive Relationships Between the Sower, the Seed, and the Soil

Each character or component that is featured in the parable of preeminence is closely intertwined:

1. **The sower sows the seed indiscriminately** – Christ does not indicate that the sower shows a preference regarding where the seed is sown. Instead, He simply states that the sower sows the seed and allows it to fall where it may.
2. **The seed is viable** – Clearly, the seed being sown is able to produce, as indicated by the fact that in three of the four soil types, it produces. The life span of the plants produced in each soil type is not a function of the seed but of the condition of the soil where it was sown.
3. **The soil is viable but possesses varying degrees of potential** – Clearly, the soil is viable and possesses enough strength (in terms of its nutrients and water content) to produce. However, only one soil type possesses the ability to sustain growth.

These are the main points of the parable for a kingdom citizen to understand:

- Your sower (the preacher sent with the Word) must have seed to sow. Without it, you cannot survive.

- The seed must be the Word of God in order to produce a harvest.
- The soil (your heart) must receive the seed (the anointed Word) in order to produce.
- The seed (the Word) must be protected from the bird (Satan, the thief and destroyer).
- The sower (the preacher sent with the Word) and the soil (your life that must be productive for the kingdom) must have a symbiotic, mutually exclusive relationship in order for both to fulfill the will of God in their lives.

In His explanation of the spiritual meaning of this parable, Christ indicated that specific relationships exist between the sower, the seed, and the soil. He also indicated that the bird's goal is to interfere in these interactive relationships. Thus, the bird, which is symbolic of Satan, is in conflict with the sower (the preacher/teacher) and acts on the seed (the Word of God) to initiate this conflict. In short, the sower's job is to sow seed, and the bird's job is to prevent the soil from receiving the seed—seems straightforward enough. However, this interaction is not the only source of conflict in the parable. Latent conflict also exists within the soil itself (which we know Satan participates in, yet not as a bird). The seed relies on the viability of the soil. Without viable soil, the seed cannot produce. The Greek word for "bird" in the parable of preeminence is *peteinon*. *Peteinon* [<pet-i-non'>, (πετεινόν)] is derived from the Greek word *etomai*, which means "to fly or winged." Thus, by definition, we know that the bird (Satan) has wings and can fly. Always remember, Satan comes for the Word's sake! Every time you get a Word from God, Satan comes for it! He knows that if you allow God's Word to germinate in your life, it can produce a thirty-, sixty-, or a hundred-fold outcome that will build God's kingdom and cause destruction to his own! Therefore, when Satan attacks, he is not coming to attack your relationship, your finances, or your career; ultimately, he is coming to steal what the sower has taught you about God and His faithfulness! He is coming for the seed—the WORD. Satan does not attack people; he attacks seed. Thus, if you do not have any Word going on in your life and you say the devil is attacking you, you are wrong! The devil comes only for the Word's sake, so if you are not holding onto the Word, you don't have anything he wants. The challenges you are going through are simply the consequences of bad decisions you have made—not attacks of the devil!

In order to convey the spiritual mysteries of the kingdom of God to people who were only familiar with an earthly kingdom structure in an agrarian economy, Christ relied upon parables—using common examples that were easily understood to those living in the first century. Their ability to readily recognize and interpret kingdom principles and dynamics was paramount to the disciples' ability to perpetuate the message of the kingdom. The most fundamental and essential of these parables is the parable of the sower—the parable of preeminence.

Individual/Soil Type	Description/Limiting Condition
Wayside Ground	Hard-hearted and emotionally/spiritually damaged believers
Stony Ground	Spiritually shallow, fair-weather believers
Thorny Ground	Spiritually careless and easily distracted believers
Good Ground	Believers who recognize God's agenda, respect the Word, remember God's expectations, remain focused, respond in faith, and remain faithful

Your Life in the Kingdom

Now let me talk plainly and simply about your new life in the kingdom. When you gave your life to Christ by the power of the Holy Spirit, you confessed Him as Lord or King and He who saved you from your sin nature and its consequence as your personal Savior. Once you were born again, you should have been able to see the kingdom, enter the sphere of the kingdom through the supernatural powers of God, and then seek the kingdom culture, practices, and principles for the rest of your earthly existence. You were then granted a spiritual birth certificate, and your name was written in the Lamb's Book of Life, registering your citizenship in heaven. Thus, you became a citizen of the kingdom of God, and now you must serve in the embassy, or the church, of the living God.

So let's look at it simply. You gave your life to Christ, and you became a part of a local embassy, the church. When you became a part of the local embassy, you were placed under the charge and leadership of the fivefold ministry gifts, and their role is to ensure your spiritual growth and development through discipleship. Now here it is—you are a part of the church; you know you joined a church in order to serve God and learn your faith while sharing it with others. Prayerfully, the local church you chose is a reflection of Christ's kingdom. The church is responsible for unlocking the practices, principles, and culture of the kingdom through the teaching ministries within it. Christ stated that the church had been given the "keys to the kingdom," so it is the church's responsibility to teach you the kingdom, and it is your responsibility to learn how to live as a kingdom citizen.

When it comes to entering, living, and expanding the kingdom, it can be overwhelming if you don't have some type of rubric that assists you in your journey. This is what excites me so about the ministry of Jesus: He provided for us what I believe is the number one key to living a victorious kingdom life. Jesus taught many, many parables on the kingdom of God, but He specifically taught us which parable would be most advantageous to our kingdom maturity and development. That parable is the parable of preeminence or the parable of the sower. In the parable of the sower lies the foundation for the basics of kingdom life. Jesus states the following about this parable and our kingdom lives: "It has been given to us to know the mystery of the kingdom of God."

When He was alone with the 12 disciples, He opened up the meaning of the parable. Christ stated that He desires for us to understand the mystery of the kingdom. The word "mystery" is a very interesting term. It has what I describe as a fraternal meaning. When I was in college, I pledged a Greek fraternity, Kappa Alpha Psi. Kappa Alpha Psi, like the other Greek fraternities and sororities, had mystery knowledge that many were curious about, but the meaning was not shared with those who had not been inducted, sworn in, or crossed the burning sands. The term "mystery" is a Greek term that carries this same type of connotation. The Greek word is *mustérion* (μυστήριον), noun from *mustés*, "a person initiated into sacred mysteries," which is from *mueó*, "to initiate, learn a secret; a secret, or esoteric knowledge."[29] The term denotes something hidden and made known only by revelation. In Matthew 13:11, "to them it is not given" means the mysteries of the kingdom of heaven are not revealed to them since they are not related to King Jesus. *Mustérion* denotes a spiritual truth couched under an external representation or similitude and concealed or hidden unless some explanation is given, as represented in Mark 4:11 and Luke 8:10.[30]

The kingdom is a mystery to those who are on the outside but not to those who are on the inside; the kingdom ought to be made plain and simple. Thus, Jesus stated to you it has been given [Greek (δίδωμι) *didómi*, which means "to give of one's own accord and with

---

[29] Spiros Zodhiates, The Complete Word Study Dictionary: New Testament (electronic ed.), (Chattanooga, TN: AMG Publishers, 2000).
[30] Ibid.

good will"] to know the mystery of the kingdom. Those who are in the kingdom should know [Greek *ginóskó* (γινώσκω), "to know, in a beginning sense, that is, to come to know, to gain or receive a knowledge of, to know in a completed sense"[31]] the mystery of the kingdom. The point here is that Jesus provides insight into the kingdom to those who have embraced Him. As kingdom citizens, there are things that are available for your understanding that others on the outside cannot understand.

The parable of the sower is the mother of all parables. This parable teaches us that the kingdom life involves four primary areas:

- **Sower** – In this parable, Christ is the sower who preaches and teaches the Word of God, and the sower is also represented by those whom Christ sends (Ephesians 4:11) with the message. If you are going to understand the kingdom, you must understand the significance of the sower. The Bible asks how one can hear without a preacher (Romans 10:14). Never allow yourself to think negatively about your sower, because the enemy will use this against you in a major way!
- **Seed** – The seed represents the Word of God. In this parable, Jesus is explaining that the sower and the seed are connected. You cannot get the seed in context without the sower.
- **Soil** – The soil represents the condition of the human heart when the sower is commanded to sow seed. You must learn how to manage the seasons of your life, because if you do not, you will distort your soil. If you distort your soil, the Word that could have delivered you will do nothing, and Satan will come to devour that which was meant to give you life!
- **Bird** – The bird represents Satan and his agenda, which is to steal, kill, and destroy the Word of God that comes into your life (John 10:10). He does not mind if you go to church

---

[31] Ibid.

and sleep, get confused, don't learn, repeatedly go to the restroom, etc.; as long as you don't get the Word, Satan is satisfied. When you are walking around while the Word is being preached, fidgeting with mobile devices and getting distracted, it is because the spirit of stupor has come upon you. You can't see, you can't hear, and you can't understand, and it will not change until you go to exile.

In short, remember that:

- The Sower represents Christ.
- The Seed represents the Word of God.
- The Soil represents four people types or conditions of the human heart when they hear the Word.
- The Bird represents Satan.

The relationship between these areas defines your spiritual life. When you learn how to interpret your kingdom life from this paradigm, I believe you will understand how your life functions as a kingdom citizen. Let's take a closer look at your life in the kingdom as explained by Jesus by simplifying the kingdom into the four critical variables that are outlined in the parable:

- The Sower Who Sows
- The Seed That Sits
- The Soil That Selects (free moral agency)
- Satan Who Sabotages

This parable suggests that in the kingdom, we must deal with the preacher, the preaching, the person, and the predator at all times!

The emphasis of the text is how each person type or soil relates to the seed, or the Word of God, that is sown by the sower. Those who respond inappropriately don't enjoy the long-term effects of the power of the Word. Thus, this kingdom parable points out four different kingdom outcomes based upon the type of soil, or person, the Word falls upon. The parable lays out the fundamental interactions of things and persons in the kingdom and emphasizes the interaction of kingdom relationships:

- Between the Sower and the Seed
- Between the Seed and the Soil
- Between the Seed and Satan
- Between the Sower and the Soil

These areas and their interactions represent the active dynamics of kingdom life.

Chapter Seven
The Sower

T HE FIRST AREA THAT a kingdom citizen must be sensitive to and understand is the sower. A sower is a very important person in Israel; ancient Israel was an agrarian culture that depended greatly upon the soil for its survival. A sower was a primary occupation in an agrarian culture. Soil was so important that God had Sabbath laws that protected the land. During the proper seasons, the sower would emerge with a bag wrapped around his shoulder full of seed, prepared to sow seed for the harvest. The sower would till the ground to make it easier for the seed to take root; the sower had to lay the groundwork before he began to sow the seed to increase the probabilities of the seed yielding a harvest. The expected outcome of the sower was a harvest! The harvest was the return on investment of the sower's seeds. The sower would sow seed indiscriminately and consistently, ensuring that he sowed seed throughout the entire field. The sower had to work the ground in order to get a high yield; then he would use a plow in order to bury the seed.

In short, in ancient Palestine, the work of the sower was as follows:

- Break up the ground.
- Sow the seed into the ground.
- Cover the seed.

The analogy is that the sower had to work with the ground before he sowed the seed. In the kingdom, the sower has to make the heart and soul of the individual ready before the impartation of the Word of God. The sower must work with the soil (human heart) before he can effectively sow seed (Word of God). In the kingdom, the preacher must understand the necessity of pre-work; when it comes time to preach or teach the Word, there has to be some groundwork to prepare people's hearts for the Word. Both the sower and the soil have to prepare themselves for the sowing of the Word.

When you are in the kingdom, you must be conscientious at a very early age of the dynamics of the sower and the seed. The sower is placed in the kingdom for the soil to yield spiritual fruit or increase. The King places the sower in the kingdom with a mission of sowing seed. In the parable, Jesus reveals both the importance of the sower and the work of the sower. The sower's main function is to sow seed; thus, he must do so indiscriminately, expecting a harvest in the future. He must also do so by faith, not being overly concerned about the elements or the birds that eat the seed. The sower must believe God that the seed will take root and produce. The work of the sower is extensive and includes everything from watching and praying for the soil and providing it with knowledge and understanding to making soil adjustments.

The work of the sower is:

- **To gather seed and hear from God (Acts 6)** – Because spending time in the Word and with God in prayer is the sower's primary responsibility, the deacons' ministry was created in Acts 6. During this time in the New Testament church, the apostles were doing too much of the menial labor, and it was taking away from their time of prayer and study of the Word. The deacons ensured that the apostles were not overworked in menial tasks.

- **To watch and pray for the soil (Hebrews 13:17)** – The sower will always keep his eye on the soil because he must give an account for them. He pulls up weeds, wards off predators, and ensures their spiritual wellbeing.

- **To provide knowledge and understanding (Jeremiah 3:15)** – The sower is responsible for feeding the soil with knowledge (what you know) and understanding (the ability to implement what you have learned). If you come to church or Bible study week after week and take notes, but never put into practice what you've learned, you've simply wasted your time and not grown in understanding.

- **To equip the soil for productivity (Ephesians 4:12)** – The sower is charged with equipping the saints for the work of ministry, training them to fulfill their work of ministry and then putting them in the proper place to be able to exercise their ministry gifts in such a way that they will bring a yield for the kingdom.

- **To make soil adjustments (Matthew 18:15–20, Hebrews 12:7–11)** – A sower must continually measure and monitor the condition of the soil. Sometimes it has to have a little fertilizer added to it before it can produce some good growth. For example, Matthew 18 talks about having conflict and how to solve it. Hebrews 12 says that if you are without correction, then you are illegitimate and not sons. A sower's job is to be able to go to the soil and say, "You are out of God's will, and if you keep this up, you will backslide and not even know that you are backslidden." Most people cannot deal with soil adjustments, so if their soil is messed up, it will be messed up for life. Unadjusted soil will not change; it will exercise the option of finding another church that is open at all times.

- **To model Christ (1 Corinthians 11:1, Hebrews 13:7)** – The sower is responsible for modeling Christ for the soil. Paul says that his disciples should follow him as he followed Christ. Hebrews 13 says to remember your leaders and imitate their faith. Thus, the soil is not supposed to look at its leader and say, "Wow! You're a wonderful man of God, Pastor. You do it! I really appreciate your zeal and your commitment to the things of God. Better you than me!" The sower is a model! You are not supposed to look at him or her and simply admire him or her—if you do, you don't understand the kingdom. You are to imitate him! Even Jesus said that these works that I do, greater works will you do because I go to the Father (John 14:12). He did not come so that we could say, "He was exemplary, wasn't He?" Christ was the model, not for us to watch but for us to follow! Likewise, the sower is the model for us to follow. If you see the sower sacrificing, you are supposed to sacrifice! If you see the sower walking in faith, you walk in faith!

The world of the kingdom is established on the earth through the church, and the fivefold ministry governs the church. When you are born again, you see the necessity of the sower when you enter into a relationship with Christ and His church. Thus, you submit yourself to a spiritual covenant with the sower or shepherd, who is responsible for soil management and maintenance. In the kingdom, the kingdom citizen does not have an anti-establishment or anti-church attitude but realizes that the church is the possession of Christ and is staffed by the person Jesus selects to lead the kingdom church through Ephesians 4:10–11.

The work of the sower is to produce a yield; the sower shows up for ministry purposes to produce spiritual yield. The soil is expected to produce a yield for both the primary sower, Christ (and disciples), and the secondary sower, the fivefold ministry gift (financial blessings). The soil is dependent upon the primary sower and the secondary sower. As a result, it is responsible for producing a yield for both the primary sower and the secondary sower.

- **Primary Sower** – According to John 15:8, the yield for the primary sower is discipleship. For the seed that Christ sows, He expects disciples to be made. If you do not make any disciples, Christ is yielding nothing out of your life. If no one is getting saved off of your life, no matter how much you say you "talk to people all the time about Jesus," you are not doing kingdom work. Simply put, real kingdom work produces disciples.

- **Secondary Sower** – The secondary yield is for the sent sower or apostolic gift. According to Galatians 6:6, the soil that is seeded with the Word should share all good things with the sower. "Sharing all good things" means to bless the sower monetarily, not simply bless him with kind words. Every time you get a financial blessing, your sower is supposed to get a blessing. Why? Because God blessed you to be productive and get an increase, and it was the sower who preached the Word that caused you to be productive. Thus, he deserves part of the increase. The sower is so important; his work is a divine assignment. Those to whom he is called to sow the seed of the Word are responsible for ensuring that he is taken care of just like God had Israel take care of the Levitical priesthood.

Sowing, Reaping, and Sharing in the Increase

As parents, you expect that one day, if your children do well, because of what you have sown into their lives, you will get a return! In the same way, because of the sower's sacrifices, when we are blessed, he expects to get a return—that is his yield off of our lives. God is not mocked, for whatsoever a man sows that shall he also reap (Galatians 6:6–8). If you get taught the Word, you keep your mind and you become productive, all as a result of the work of the sower. Thus, the sower deserves to share in your increase! If you selfishly keep everything you yield and choose to use it on yourself rather than recycle some of it back to the teacher, you will reap corruption of the flesh. However, if you remember your leaders when you are blessed with a yield, you will reap life everlasting. Why would you think that you are supposed to be financially blessed, but your leaders should not be?

Keep in mind that allowing your teacher to share in your increase is not about bringing your tithes and offerings; it is about bringing special gifts directly to the sower. When we bring these gifts, Philippians 4:19 assures us that the God of the sower will meet the needs of the one that sows. The soil is responsible for praying for, recognizing, esteeming, and supporting the sower, and this is to the soil's benefit because it should never want anything to hinder or distract the sower from sowing the seed into its life (1 Corinthians 9:9–13). Since we understand how important sowers are to our lives, we should pray for them, recognize them, esteem them, and support and assist them wherever and however we can (1 Thessalonians 5:12–13). The very last thing that you should ever want is for your sower to be down, be distracted, be in lack, or feel unsupported and unappreciated. Why? Because you never want anything to get in the way of him sowing the seed into your life. You need that seed to live, and you need it to be productive in life, so you must look after the sower!

When you are a law-abiding kingdom citizen, you have high regard for spiritual authority. The kingdom citizen understands that kingdom operations involve kingdom protocol and the order of things, and in the kingdom, God establishes His church as the entity to represent His kingdom upon the earth. The King also calls and sovereignly chooses those who will be divine representatives of the kingdom through the formal offices of the church. The kingdom citizen understands the necessity of getting off the couch and being on the front lines of ministry while serving in the local church under the spiritual care, protection, and instruction of the sower. Kingdom citizens remember and think about their leaders, understanding it is the sower's spiritual work that establishes their spiritual future.

Kingdom citizens' first area of recognition of criticality in the kingdom is that the sower sows the seed they need! When you enter the kingdom, you should look for and expect a constant word from the King through an appointed and anointed sower who has been called to preach the kingdom, teach the kingdom, and demonstrate the kingdom. The kingdom begins with God's selection for leadership, and that leadership is responsible for preaching and teaching the Word of God in such a way that you are equipped to do the will of God personally for your life and expand the kingdom's influence in your world. Let me have a kingdom talk with you. Kingdom citizens understand that when you enter the kingdom, you come into your spiritual life as a new infant who desires the sincere milk of the word (1 Peter 2:2). The most important people to new kingdom citizens are their parents—their heavenly Father and their spiritual father.

As a kingdom citizen, you must appreciate your spiritual leader because it is his role to teach you the kingdom. Your natural sower or fivefold ministry gift sower is responsible for teaching you the Word. Thus, when you become a kingdom citizen, you must walk in kingdom protocol. In the parable, Jesus explains the role of the sower who sows the seed. The sower represents Christ as the supreme and ultimate sower, but the kingdom principle is that in the kingdom, the role of the shepherd is to sow the Word of God. Any kingdom ambassador who is on assignment for the King desires to teach the Word, not simply pacify people. In the kingdom, you will always find a sower. Your pastor is your sower, and Christ was the original Sower.

The Sower Sows (Romans 10:14–17, Jeremiah 3:15, 2 Timothy 4:2)

The sower preaches and teaches the Word of God, not motivational speeches, not messages that border on secular humanism, but a life-changing word that is rooted in God's Word! The sower is what is referred to in the Old Testament as the *shaluach*: he who speaks the

Word; the one who has been sent. The *shaluach* is the representative of the King. Whenever God gets ready to do something, he raises up someone to lead the charge. The word "apostle" is a very interesting word; it comes from the Greek word *apostolos*, which comes from the Greek word *apostelló*, which is translated from the Hebrew word, חַלֵשׁ *shaluach*, which means "to send a messenger or representative." The word *apostelló* is translated over 700 times in the Septuagint from the word *shaluach*. Intertestamental literature states that a *shaluach* or messenger is not one simply with mechanical orders but one who exercises the rights and authority of his sender. The *shaluach* was authorized to conduct business on behalf of his sender; he possessed the power of attorney. The Mishnah (the oral traditions of the rabbis) stated that a man's *shaluach* was said to be as the man himself; he could actually represent a man at his wedding, and it would legal and binding. However, he could not consummate or have sexual activity with the bride. The *shaluach* had authority to conduct business on behalf of the one who sent him.

The kingdom citizen must have a kingdom perspective about spiritual leaders in order to understand they are not just men and women; they are God's official representatives. Therefore the *shaluach* or *apostolos* is God's choice to do business on His behalf. The most important person in your life is your sower. When God anoints the sower, he comes ready to sow. He has been dispatched or sent with cargo from heaven for you. How beautiful are the feet of them who preach the gospel (Romans 10:15). There is a relationship between the sower, seed, and soil. The soil depends on the seed, who depends on the sower. Apart from the sower, you cannot do what God has called you to do. The sower is God's representative of the kingdom of God for you on Earth.

Chapter Eight
The Seed

I N THE PREVIOUS CHAPTER, we established that the kingdom's primary player is the sower (Jesus) and then His secondary sower is the fivefold ministry gift responsible for preparing the soil for the sowing of the seed. He is also responsible for sowing the seed into the ground. The kingdom citizen never disrespects, neglects, or ignores the office or the work of the sower. What makes the sower so special, aside from being God's official messenger, is what he or she carries—the seed. In this chapter, we want to discuss the kingdom and the seed.

The seed is the central focus of the parable and the kingdom. Although the most valuable character of the parable is the sower, because he represents the primary sower and His agenda, the seed is the central place of conflict. Jesus, who is the primary sower, did not simply represent God as one who dispersed the Word of God but was Himself the Word. John 1 states that in the beginning was the Word, the Word was with God, and the Word was God. John goes on to state that the Word became flesh and dwelled among us (1:14). What makes everything happen in this parable is the Word of God; likewise, everything in the kingdom revolves around the Word of God. What makes a church a legitimate church or embassy of the kingdom is that it is the place where people can hear and learn the Word of God. If the church is not the heralder of the Scriptures, it is not an official church. The church is called to be the pillar and ground/foundation of truth (1 Timothy 3:15). The sower is the sower because he has the seed; the church is the church because it is the ground of truth or the Word of God. When you enter the kingdom, you understand what makes your shepherd so valuable is his role and connection to the seed.

Let's take a closer look at the seed and the kingdom culture based upon our parable. Once again, the sower is a first century Palestinian farmer who lives in an agrarian culture, and the main industry of that day was farming. Everyone depended upon the fruit of farming for their physical existence; it was how they received their crop of wheat and vegetables, etc. Everyone depended upon the work of the sower; he had universal importance. As quiet as it is kept, the farmer is still critical to the health and the physical existence of our contemporary society. While modern farming methods have changed, agriculture remains a dominant sector of the Palestinian economy as it employs much of the population and is a major component of their current gross domestic product.

The first century farmer initially prepared his field by plowing manually or with the assistance of a large animal. Plowing was necessary to turn over the upper layer of the soil, bringing fresh nutrients to the surface while burying weeds, allowing them to break down and aerate the soil to hold moisture better. Plowing produces a series of linear cuts in the soil, called furrows. The field is then seeded through a process called manual broadcasting. In this method, the farmer throws seeds over the field indiscriminately. The seeds that land on the furrows has better protection from the elements, weeds, bird consumption, and natural erosion. The seeds that land outside the furrows do not have as much potential for growth as the seeds that land on plowed ground.

The function of the sower is sowing the seed; the function of the seed is producing crops. However, the contingency of the success of these functions is the type of soil the seed lands on. This was all common knowledge to Christ's audience when He taught this parable to them. People in antiquity valued the sower because their life depended upon his work. His work depended upon having viable seeds, and his seeds were organic products of the original thing that was desired. The seed was vitally important for reproduction of vital nutrients that were produced from the soil of the earth.

Genesis 8:22 says, "*While the earth remains, seedtime and harvest, cold and heat, winter and summer, and day and night shall not cease.*" The culture of seedtime and harvest is a kingdom culture that is inherent in this parable and describes life in the kingdom as a kingdom citizen. You are provided a sower who has the necessary seeds to plant in the soil of your heart that will produce the necessary harvest out of your soil.

Now let's look at the seed. In this parable, Christ lets us know that the seed is representative of the Word of God (Luke 8:11). There are two Greek words commonly translated as "word." The first is *logos*, which speaks of the general Word of God (written Word), and the second is *rhema*, which speaks of the specific word contained in the *logos* that is God's will for your life. John is writing to a primarily Greek audience and a Hellenistic culture in Ephesus. Therefore, John writes definitively that Christ is the divine *logos*, a concept that was readily understood in that culture. He writes to a culture that is enveloped in thought and reason and defines Christ as the mind and thoughts of God among men.

In antiquity, it was assumed that the seed that the sower was to sow was good seed; thus, the focus in the parable is not the authenticity or effectiveness of the seed, but the focus is upon the type of soil in which the seed lands. The seed, which is the Word of God, is always good, regardless of the type of soil it falls upon. Jesus teaches us that the Word of God is only functional on the soil that receives it. If the soil is receptive, the seed can produce. Thus, the Word is efficacious in the life of all who receive it. The Word has the power to produce and never loses that power. Even when we are not productive in our lives, it is not because the Word lacks the power to produce. This is better understood by looking at the Hebrew language.

The Hebrew word commonly translated "word" is *dabar*. By definition, *dabar* means "word, matter, or thing." This definition informs us that whatever the Word is sent to produce is actually housed within the Word itself. It does not have to get something from an external source. Housed within the Word is everything needed to bring the Word to pass. We see this plainly in biblical accounts of creation. The author of Hebrews tells us that the entire physical world was framed by the invisible Word of God (Hebrews 11:3), and that invisible Word continues to sustain everything in existence (Hebrew 1:3). The Genesis account of creation shows us that God's vehicle for forming creation as a whole was through a spoken Word. God's creation was not assembled from preexisting material but from the very Word that He spoke. The beloved Apostle John informs us that all things were made by the Word (John 1:1–3). The way that the Word works hasn't changed! The Word works the same way in the life of believers today as it did in creation. He is the same God who speaks a Word, and that Word has potential, power, purpose, and production, and it performs the will of God. The Word of God can change any situation in your life and does not need a pre-existing circumstance to do so. Simply put, the Word is self-sufficient.

The Hebrew root from which *dabar* is derived from is *dabara*, which means "to be behind or to back." This word implies that God is behind His Word, pushing it through (Jeremiah 1:12). The meanings of the two Hebrew words, *dabar* and *dabara*, lead us to conclude that whatever we need is not only resident in the Word, but that God also backs His Word to ensure that it produces. This definition makes the Word both practical and powerful in our lives because it is self-sufficient, backed by God Himself, and spoken directly to us. This power of the Word, which spoke darkness into light, is the same power of the Word that speaks productivity into our lives for His glory.

The Bible States the Following About the Word	
The Word of God is the expressed thoughts of God.	John 1:1
The Word of God is truth.	John 17:17
The Word of God is the creative force of God.	Genesis 1:1
The Word of God is the incorruptible life giver.	1 Peter 1:23
The Word of God is the discerner of thoughts and intents.	Hebrews 4:12
The Word of God is the source of healing.	Psalm 107:20
The Word of God is the sustaining power of the universe.	Hebrews 1:3
The Word of God is that which performs His will.	Isaiah 55:10–11

The most valuable character of this kingdom parable is the Word of God, the seed. It is the seed that gives the sower importance in the parable, it is the seed that is necessary for the soil to produce, and it is the seed for which the bird comes.

The kingdom citizen understands that the most valuable kingdom commodity that they possess is the seed. In the kingdom, people constantly desire to hear a Word from the King. Kingdom citizens are first trying to hear the written Word, then the spoken Word, then the prophetic word, then a word of knowledge. The Word of God contains your next level breakthrough! You must learn to passionately desire the Word of God. Jesus said that just as important as bread or food is in one's life, the Word of God is more important, for man does not live by bread alone (Matthew 4:4). As the deer pants toward the water brook, the believer must seek after the Word of God. Kingdom citizens understand that a word in season is the foundation of spiritual breakthrough and transformation. However, kingdom citizens are not the only ones who understand the power of the Word; Satan does also. Satan desires to take the Word from your life or make it difficult for it to be productive in your life.

The Word of God is your offensive weapon against Satan. The Word of God is all that he recognizes and respects, so he desires to take your sword. The Word of God should be in your mouth as a two-edged sword as a weapon against him. As long as you remain ignorant or satisfied with not knowing the Word or saying the Bible is confusing, he knows that he can have his way with you. Jesus defeated the enemy in the wilderness after a horrendous battle with temptation with the written Word, not the Mishnah but the Torah. You cannot defeat Satan with traditions; you can only defeat the enemy with the Word of God. Why? The Word of God is alive, quick, and more powerful than a two-edged sword (Hebrews 4:12).

The sower sows the Word! Thus, in kingdom worship, believers revolve their lives around the Word and the dictates in the Word. During the week, there are weekday Bible studies; during the week, people are desiring the Word daily and ordering their conduct aright according to the Word; and on Sundays, the saints gather to worship God corporately according to the Word. The early church met from house to house daily, and the book of Acts says that the Word spread mightily. The first two variables in the kingdom are the sower and the seed. Thus, if you want to live a victorious life in the kingdom, make sure you are sitting under a kingdom sower who is sowing the Word of God into your life with a kingdom focus—not a church focus, not a social focus, not a cultural focus, not a neighborhood focus, and not a personal focus but a kingdom focus. The Word of God is designed to produce the will of God in the lives of the soils that it falls upon. Our faith is built when we are learning the Word of God and governing our lives according to His will. Thus, we understand the veracity of Paul's words to the church in Rome:

> *How then shall they call on Him in whom they have not believed? And how shall they believe in Him of whom they have not heard? And how shall they hear without a preacher? ...So then faith comes by hearing, and hearing by the word of God.*[32]

---

[32] Romans 10:14, 17

Chapter Nine
The Soil

E VERY KINGDOM CITIZEN MUST understand the roles that the preacher and the preached Word play in their life. No one can truly become what the King has designed them to become until they connect with the Word in such an intimate way that they need it daily in order to survive.

The third kingdom variable that the parable of preeminence teaches us about is the soil. As stated, the most important character in this parable is the seed, and everyone and everything in the parable revolves around the seed. The sower is defined by the seed—if the preacher is preaching popular thought or humanistic principles rather than the Scriptures, then it is clear that he is not a kingdom sower. The kingdom sower must be connected to the Word of the King, not the word of popular thought. The Word defines the sower, not the sower the Word. The Word is the most valuable emphasis of the parable; it is what Satan desires to take, and it is what the soil needs to be productive. Let's take a closer look at the soil.

Remember that the hearers of this parable understood that the plowed furrows represent only a portion of the field's area and that their broadcasting efforts distributed seeds evenly across the field. Thus, they understood that their crop's productivity was not dependent on the seed nor the sower but rather the condition of the soil. The four soils in this parable represent different dispositions of the hearers of the Word (seed) as it is being sown. God made humankind from the dust of the earth (Genesis 2:7); thus, we are the soil in this parable. Every time we hear the Word, however, Christ describes that we can be in one of four states of receptivity for the seed or Word: wayside, stony, thorny, or good ground.

In farming, tillage encourages soil receptivity. Tillage is the agricultural preparation of the soil by agitation of various types, such as digging, stirring, and overturning. Tilled soil is able to receive seeding better than other soil types. Plowing serves three distinct functions:

1. It overturns the soil, killing the current vegetation.
2. It breaks up the soil so that air can get to the roots of the plants and rain can soak the ground.
3. It turns over the soil so that weed seeds are buried deep in the ground and killed (weeds compete with the plants for water, air, and light to grow), and the crop seeds are buried on top for greater growth potential.

Tilling speaks to the preparation of one's heart to receive the Word. Contrary to popular thought, it takes preparation to properly hear the Word of God. This is because the Word often challenges our current way of thinking and requires us to perform faith-filled actions. The Word requires us to change—in Jeremiah, God said that it is like a hammer that breaks the rock in pieces (Jeremiah 23:29). Thus, in order to hear and accept the Word of God, we have to prepare ourselves to embrace change.

Change is not always easy to accept, as it requires us to first assess and then discard the behaviors, thinking patterns, and habits that have produced the undesirable results with which we are currently faced. Thus, change requires that we own up to our waywardness and humble ourselves in correction—change requires repentance.

If we are not ready to repent at the rebuke of the Word, then we are not ready to receive the transformation that comes with the Word. The Apostle Paul, in his second epistle to his ministry son, Timothy (2 Timothy 3:16–17), writes, *"All scripture is given by inspiration of God, and is profitable for doctrine, for reproof, for correction, for instruction in righteousness: that the man of God may be complete, thoroughly equipped for every good work."* Paul's view of the Word in this text is counter to the view of many modern preachers that frame the Word of God in encouraging and inspirational stories. Yes, the Word can inspire and encourage (soil needs water then light to grow), but if it's going to transform our lives and make us more productive in the kingdom, we must also embrace the correction (breaking up) and instruction (weed control) that is resident within it.

Tilling is the preparation of the ground to receive the seed. Agriculturalists, since the beginning of time, have learned the importance of creating good soil to produce a beautiful crop. The positive effects are:

- Tilling loosens and aerates the soil, which can facilitate some deeper penetration of roots.
- Tilling helps in the even mixing of residue from the harvest, organic matter (humus), and nutrients throughout the soil.
- Tilling helps to destroy weeds.

Tilling was first performed via human labor, sometimes involving slaves. Hoofed animals could also be used to till soil via trampling. The wooden plow was then invented; it could be pulled by a mule, ox, elephant, water buffalo, or similarly sturdy animal. The steel plow allowed tilling in the American Midwest to be a little easier, breaking up tough prairie grasses and rocks. Soon after 1900, the farm tractor was introduced, which eventually made modern large-scale agriculture possible.[33]

---

[33] Wikipedia, "Tillage," Retrieved from https://en.wikipedia.org/wiki/Tillage.

As Jesus told the parable of the sower (the parable of preeminence), He directed the attention of the people to a sower sowing off in the distance. The multitudes that listened to Him teach were from an agrarian culture, so there were certain things that were already built in to their understanding when He began to teach using this example. Automatically, there were certain things He did not have to explain. The culture inherently understood that there were four types of soil that the sower encountered when he went out to sow. In this parable, the four soil types represent the four types of conditions or spiritual states that someone's heart can be in when he or she hears the seed of the Word being sown. Let's examine the four soils:

1. **Wayside ground** – An impenetrable path that the sower walked on in order to sow the seed, this was the beaten path that was so trodden that it was not good for receiving the seed.

2. **Stony ground** – In ancient Palestine, some of the field had limestone covered with small layers of dirt that prohibited it from establishing deep roots. When a seed fell on this soil, it only developed shallow roots.

3. **Thorny ground** – This was dirt full of weeds that competed for the soil's resources and choked out the desired crop.

4. **Good ground** – Good soil was soil that had been properly tilled and prepared for the deposit of the seed—quality soil that produced thirty-, sixty-, and a hundred-fold harvest increases.

These are the four types of ground that were present when the ancient Palestinian sower sowed seed. Each of these types of soils represent the four possible hearts and attitudes that people may have during the sowing of the seed of the Word. Although these four types of ground represent the state of a person's heart, they are not relegated to being this type of ground permanently; thus, no person's soil state or condition is fixed or permanent. Anyone can make a choice to be good ground at any time. For example, while hearing one message, a person may choose to be attentive and alert by listening intently, staying focused, and taking notes and making a resolution to implement the principles that were taught into his or her life. This is being good ground. In another message, the same person may decide to be disinterested, tune out, and even allow himself or herself to fall asleep, thus becoming wayside ground. At any time during the message, however, they have the ability to choose to be good ground.

Jesus is teaching us kingdom fundamentals in this parable. When you enter into the kingdom, you should first encounter the King and the King's representative, who travels with a Word from God or seeds of the kingdom. The kingdom citizen understands that both the sower and the seed exist in order to get the production of God out of their life as the soil of God. So you have to ask yourself this question every time the Word of God is being preached: What kind of soil am I? As mentioned, whatever your attitude is when the Word is being preached can change, or you may remain consistent in how you respond to the Word. For example, some people always tap out when the Word is being taught: they text, look at Facebook, or engage in some other outside activity. Others always are attentive to the Word and listen, but you still have others who sometimes listen and sometimes don't. However, the type of soil you are when you hear the Word preached or taught determines how victorious you will be in the kingdom. Let's take an in-depth look at the four soils and the one that most describes your behavior in the kingdom of God.

The Wayside Ground
Even though this person sits under and hears the preached Word, the wayside ground is completely unresponsive to the Word of God. This person's response to the Word is "You keep a-knocking, but you can't come in!" The wayside ground represents that which does not respond to God when it hears the Word; the preached message has no impact on this person's life. After this person leaves the

environment, they do not understand the Word, they do not believe the Word, and even though they heard the Word, they do nothing with it—the Word will not be acted upon. Thus, the wayside ground is completely unresponsive to the Word of God, for it has absolutely no impact in or on their life. Even though he knows that some of his seed will fall on the hard, compact wayside ground that will not allow the seed to penetrate it and produce an increase, the sower must continue to sow indiscriminately onto all soil types.

Wayside soil is so hard that the seed cannot penetrate it. It is no wonder that the Word does not have any impact on the life of a person who is wayside ground. Wayside soil was that which the sower walked upon while he was sowing seed. It was hard and compact, so it was not fertile. As he walked along this pathway of hard-packed soil, the first century Palestinian farmer would reach into the bag of seed around his neck, grab a handful of seed, and cast the seed onto the soil upon which he intended to plant. While doing so, however, some of the seed would inadvertently fall out of his hands and onto the soil. Even though seed fell onto the wayside soil, the sower would not expect anything to grow on it. Its condition did not allow for growth. Thus, while he did not sow seed on the wayside ground intentionally, he knew that some of the seed would be unintentionally sown there anyway. The message in this is that God calls for seed to be indiscriminately sown onto all types of soil even though He knows that certain people will not listen or allow the Word to penetrate their hearts. Regardless of how receptive preachers think that listeners will be, they are still commanded to preach to people that will not hear.

People who are wayside ground are spiritually unproductive because as soon as the seed is sown, the enemy immediately comes to steal it away. Therefore, there is no growth or productivity since the seed sits right on top of the soil! The spiritual reality of the person who hears the Word but never allows it to penetrate his heart is spiritual unproductivity. Remember, the soil needs the seed in order to be productive, and since the wayside soil is so hard and compact, it is impossible for the seed to penetrate it. When the seed is sown, it simply sits on top of the wayside ground and stays there until the bird swoops down and takes it away; it eats the seed up! Because the devil knows that there will be plenty of seed sitting on top of the soil of the heart of the person who is wayside ground, he is always looming overhead waiting for the seed to be sown. As soon as the seed is sown onto this person's soil, the bird immediately comes to steal it. Thus, Satan loves people who are wayside ground. They easily give up the seed! When you are in the kingdom, you must understand how important it is to pay close attention to the sower and the seed. Every time the Word is being taught, you must be attentive because this is the time when God is trying to transform your life and Satan is trying to deform your future.

The Stony Ground
In Palestine, stony ground was characterized by a thin layer of soil over a rocky limestone layer that blocked the plant from developing deep roots to access water and nutrients; as a result, the hot sun could easily scorch the shallow plant, and it would die. If seed fell upon this type of soil, it would start to grow; however, because of the hard limestone underneath the dirt, when it started spreading out its roots, this growth would be blocked. As a result, the plant could not reach the deeper sources of water and soil nutrients that it needed to survive. This resulted in a small plant with shallow growth; it lacked depth. Consequently, when the hot sun came out, the heat from the sun would scorch up the plant, and it would wither away and die.

Those who are stony ground are considered to have impulsive hearts. Impulsive people are those who are quick to act without taking the necessary time to think all the way through these actions or the implications of their actions as well as the sustainability of what they have decided to do. So it is with people with impulsive hearts when they hear the Word: They immediately react to what they hear, and while they start out well, they do not develop the depth that is necessary to sustain their growth. Then, when the heat and the pressures of life hit them, because their growth is so shallow, the heat consumes them and they wither away. The spiritual reality of the stony ground person is that because they have not developed deep spiritual growth, when the heat and pressures of life hit, they are unable to endure them because their spiritual roots are so shallow; thus, they only last for a short time.

People who are stony ground immediately jump up and receive the Word of God with gladness! They are excited about what they hear, and they are motivated by it because of what they perceive it can do for their lives. The truth is that they keep their commitment to the Word at a surface level. Those who are stony ground come around the things of God but do not take them very seriously. They never allow themselves to get deep into the things of God, opting to be surface-level church members and not deeply devoted kingdom citizens who commit their lives to hearing the Word, implementing the Word, and bearing fruit. The spiritual reality of the stony ground person is this: As a result of not allowing themselves to develop deep spiritual roots, when life's heat and pressure begin to drain them, they do not have any way to tap in to the life-sustaining water of the Holy Spirit. They are unable to pull what they need from God because their roots are not deep enough. Therefore, when these people face challenges or crises in life, instead of enduring them like a good soldier, they get discouraged and fall away from the things of God.

Stony soil people only last for a short time. Although they will seem to start out enthusiastically about the Word, because they never take time to develop deep spiritual roots, the heat of life will soon scorch them so that they only endure for a while. Eventually, the stony ground person will walk away from the things of God. The future of the stony ground person is not a good one. Initially, they appear to be growing on the outside, but in reality, on the inside, they have only a very shallow level of dedication to actually keeping the principles of the Word of God. As a result of having no spiritual depth, although they believe the Word when they hear it, get happy about it, and are able to endure for a short while, when the heat gets too hot, they are gone. They have no root, so the future of the stony ground person is bleak! When stony ground people go absent from the fellowship, you know that it is because they are "going through" (experiencing personal pressures and difficulties in life that they cannot overcome alone) yet again, and they have not developed the internal spiritual depth and resources to weather the heat.

In my pastorate, I have experienced quite of few of this type of heart condition: They blow in, blow up, and then blow out. In the kingdom, you must really consider what it is that you are choosing. You must not be surface, be desperate, and just act; you must think before you just act, counting the cost. In the kingdom, Satan wants you not to pay attention to the Word or the seed, because he knows that the sower has a word from God for you that will transform your life. He does not want that for your life and causes you to check out, not pay attention, or just be highly emotional without thought of what God is really saying.

The Thorny Ground
Some Palestinian farmers did not invest the time and energy to pull thorns/weeds up from the root, and eventually the weeds choked the life out of the good plants. So it is with spiritual people who become preoccupied by falling among thorns, allowing the thorns to choke the spiritual life out of them. Thorny ground in first century Palestine was characterized by soil that was full of weeds. Even though they knew that the weeds would be a threat to the crop they desired to plant, many of these farmers would not take the time to rid their fields of the weeds prior to sowing seed. Instead of completely uprooting the weeds of the field, Palestinian farmers would take a shortcut: they would cut off the tops of the weeds or burn the tops off of them so that the field appeared to be free of

weeds. However, the reality was that because the roots of the weeds were still just underneath the soil, the weeds were still alive. Then, when the farmer sowed seed onto the field and the plants began to grow, the weeds would wrap around the good growth and kill it! Take note that the Bible says that they "fell among" thorns, not that the thorns fell among them. This means that the thorns, or the weeds, were already there, waiting to consume the good growth! There are two warnings to be drawn from an understanding of thorny soil: Watch a lazy sower who takes shortcuts, and watch your associations—the thorns in your life!

What does a "lazy sower" look like? There are many "lazy sowers" out here! These are the kind of sowers that take shortcuts to make things appear to be a certain way without putting in the work to actually make the appearance a reality. Lazy sowers are those who preach a message that you can listen to without being convicted or challenged about being serious about the things of God. They sugarcoat the Word, making the Bible say what it does not, and lead ministries where the required commitment level is low. The fact that they are lazy sowers is not completely their fault! The reason we have lazy sowers is because we have lazy soil! The Bible says that shepherds should feed the people with knowledge and understanding; however, when the people do not receive knowledge and understanding, instead of challenging the shepherd, they remain silent. Lazy sowers do what people allow them to do. Make your preacher teach you! Make him study! Ask him to interpret things in the Bible for you; ask him where he got the interpretation from and how he knows that it is accurate. It is not disrespectful to your preacher to ask him challenging questions about the Word!

"Fell among thorns" also means you have to watch your associations; you have to guard your fellowship. Remember, Paul wrote, "a little leaven leavens the whole lump" (1 Corinthians 5:6). When you spend time with anyone, you begin to imitate their habits unconsciously;

thus, when you hang with unbelievers or carnal Christians, you become more like them in attitude and action.

Those who are thorny ground are considered to have preoccupied hearts. Preoccupied people are those who cannot focus on one main thing, because there are so many other things around them that compete for their attention. Thorny ground people are those who allow themselves to fall among the preoccupations of this world and allow them to distract them from their kingdom focus of seeking first the kingdom of God. Instead, they become misfocused by thorns whose sole purpose is to choke the life out of them and kill their spiritual lives. While thorny ground actually experienced some growth and depth, because it fell among thorns—or bad associations—it became mentally consumed with the cares of this world, the deceitfulness of riches, and the desires for other things, and these things choked the Word out of them. When believers' minds become consumed with these things, it is easy to become preoccupied with having them and distracted from living life as a focused kingdom citizen.

Those who are thorny ground are different from wayside and stony ground. Thorny ground people used to actually have good growth! However, because they did not carefully watch the associations in their lives and protect their walk with God, they allowed themselves to connect with secular-minded people—weeds and thorns—who did not have an appreciation for the things of God. In doing so, they learned to appreciate the life of the sinner and eventually took on the values and appetites of those who serve in Satan's kingdom! They allowed these thorns to choke the Word out of them. The lesson here: Watch your associations because bad company corrupts good morals, and a little leaven leavens the whole lump!

Eventually, the cares of this world, the deceitfulness of riches, and the desire for other things become more important to thorny ground people than the kingdom. They overtake them and choke out what they need to survive: the water of the Holy Spirit and the nutrients of the Word of God. As a result, the thorny ground person dies spiritually. They walk away from the things of God, and they go back to a focus on secular living. They may attend a church, but it will be one that affirms them in their secular pursuit of worldly things and does not challenge them to a sacrificial life that seeks first the kingdom of God! The thorny ground used to be really valuable in the kingdom and the church until one day they allowed Satan to place their thoughts and hearts with affection for secular things. In the kingdom, we must recognize that the enemy is always on the prowl and waiting for an avenue to return to his house and disrupt our kingdom walk. He comes continually and consistently to steal, kill, and destroy (John 10:10)!

The Good Soil

Good soil in ancient Palestine represented fertile and well-kept soil that was ripe and healthy for production. The Palestinian sower, while being indiscriminate in his sowing, was partial to good soil because of its potential. Good soil represented the highest probability for harvesting. Thus, when Jesus speaks of the four soils, the good soil is the only one that He speaks of in a favorable manner. The seed fell on four types of soil, but only one type provided the necessary conditions for the seed to maximize its potential and the soil to produce a harvest. Of course, each of the four soils represents a possible attitude and heart condition one can have when listening to or receiving the Word of God. However, it is only the good soil that is advocated to be the disposition of the kingdom citizen. In the kingdom, you must strive to have a good attitude and a good heart every time the Word of God is preached.

The first thing the parable points out for us is that the soil is "good"—the Greek word *kalos* (καλός), which means "good as to quality and character." Then it says that the good soil has the ability to "hear," which is the Greek word *akouó* (ἀκούω). *Akouó* means "to be able to hear to the point of penetration, not simply an audible sound without clarity." The parable also communicates that the good soil "receives" the Word, which is the Greek word *paradechomai* (παραδέχομαι). *Paradechomai* means "to receive, embrace with assent and obedience." Good soil doesn't fight or argue with the Word; it yields to the Word. And then, as a result of these things, the parable states that the good soil is productive, which is the Greek term *karpophoreó* (καρποφορέω). *Karpophoreó* means "to bring forth fruit; to bear fruit."

Good soil is the result of preparation. People who are good soil prepare themselves by cultivating their soil to make sure that it is in optimal condition to receive the seed, or Word of God; as a result, they always produce an increase, whether it is thirty-, sixty-, or a hundred-fold. One thing about good soil is that it will always produce a harvest at some level. Good soil is soil that is cultivated and well maintained for the purpose of producing a good crop when the seed is sown upon it. As a result, when it receives the seed, it is able to produce and sustain a crop! Spiritually, those who are good soil are those who make the necessary preparations to receive the seed of the Word each time they enter the house of God. They are consistent in their worship attendance because they know that they need the seed in order to be productive. They also participate in fellowship and service ministry in the local church. Good ground people are productive for the kingdom because they receive the Word, guard it in their hearts, and produce a spiritual manifestation of it in their lives! This soil type is a model of the heart and attitude of the kingdom citizen in relation to the seed.

Those who are good ground are considered to have prepared hearts. Prepared people are those who evaluate what is needed for productivity and effectiveness before they go into an environment or situation. They put in order and arrange whatever is necessary prior to going into the situation to ensure that these needs are met. The good ground person is one who makes the proper arrangements before going to hear the Word. They prepare by:

- Getting plenty of rest before the worship service so that they are alert to hear the Word. They don't stay up all night but see the preaching moment as a meeting with God and desire to be sharp for the meeting.
- Clearing their minds of any distractions, worries, and concerns as they enter to hear the Word.
- Expecting to receive a rhema or specific impartation of the Word for their life. Good soil shows up with an expectation that God has a word for them and that the sower will have it in their mouth.
- Bringing something to take notes with during the service to ensure that they make note of the rhema comments that God makes to them so that they don't run the risk of losing or forgetting, because they know the power of the Word and must nurture that seed.
- Purchasing the necessary books or resources to help follow along with the teachings of the sower, who is equipping the soil for the work of ministry and to ensure that they are doctrinally in line with the sower.
- Keeping themselves alert and attentive while the seed is being sown. Good soil hates interruptions and distractions that break the flow of teaching and preaching.

Good soil is intentional in preparing to receive the seed and protecting the seed once it is planted. Good soil always produces a harvest or an increase! While we know that it is the seed that makes it productive, we also know that the soil must do its part to make sure that the seed has optimal conditions under which it can grow! Thus, by preparing itself to receive the seed and guarding and nurturing the seed once it is planted, good soil yields a crop! Those who are good soil are not in a competition to produce more than their neighbors. They recognize that God has something specific for them to do, and in order to do it, they must take the seed that He has given them and produce the increase that they were designed to produce—an increase that is unique to them! If you pay attention to yourself, you can self-monitor what type of ground you are in advance. For example, if you enter the church doors complaining about how hard it was to get there, you know that you are starting out as wayside ground! Command yourself to be good soil, and prepare to experience the kingdom when the Word is sown. Those who are good soil allow the seed to fall on their good ground and eventually produce a spiritual harvest of discipleship!

The future of good soil is an ideal one because not only do they hear the Word, but they accept the Word into their lives; they embrace its principles; and they allow their lives to be nurtured, led, and guided by the Holy Spirit (the water), and as a result, the Word bears fruit in their lives! Sometimes the increase is a smaller thirty-fold increase, and sometimes the increase is a larger hundred-fold increase. Regardless of the size of the increase, the point is clear: Good soil always provides an increase! In the kingdom, increase is characterized by one primary thing: discipleship. Thus, those who are good soil make disciples!

Should sowers expect everyone that they are teaching to be good soil, or do they already understand that people will be all types of soils when they are sowing seed? A sower can expect to find people representing each type of soil in the audience to which he is sowing seed. As a rule of thumb, he can expect the audience to be comprised of the following:

25% Wayside Ground – These are the people who are sitting in the audience but hear nothing that is said. Every seed that was sown during the message sat on top of their heart because their soil was too hard to penetrate. Since the Word is just sitting there, the devil, who comes to steal the Word, swoops down like a bird and immediately devours the seed. However, even though the wayside ground was not paying attention to the Word, God will still hold him responsible for it in judgment.

25% Stony Ground – These are the people who listen to the message and get excited about it—they may even jump up, cry out, and dance around while the seed is being sown! However, while they are excited about it, they are not committed to it. As a result, they only develop a surface relationship with God. As soon as trouble hits and the heat comes or something happens to them, they are instantly depressed. They doubt God and His Word even though they started out enthusiastically. Often they will say that they need to "take a break" from the things of God while they are "going through."

25% Thorny Ground – These are the people who are listening, but as they listen, they are saying, "It doesn't take all of this!" They listen from this position because the things of God compete with their own personal desires. They can only half-listen to the Word because their minds are preoccupied with thinking of ways to realize their secular goals. While they started out being blessed by the Word, once they start hanging out with people with opposing values and priorities to God, sitting under the Word and advancing the kingdom becomes a string of time-wasting and inconvenient tasks.

25% Good Soil – These are people who sit and listen to the Word attentively, fully-engaged and taking notes—not fighting to stay awake! The good seed that is being sown will fall on this good soil and produce an increase—always. These people have a productive, kingdom-focused life.

Thus, any preacher who receives a 25% success rate or return from the Word that he preaches is doing well! Twenty-five percent of the people were ready to leave church as soon as they arrived (wayside ground). However, 75% of the people actually respected the preaching moment and received the Word at different levels.

Let's summarize before we go to the next chapter. Because the kingdom citizen is represented by the four soils, it is important for you to determine what kind of soil you are when the Word is being taught because the Word is always good!

1. The Wayside: The Unresponsive Heart (Hard-Hearted)
    a. Wayside does not understand, does not believe, and hears but doesn't act; hard heart and head
    b. Unresponsive heart: Tied to problems
2. Stony Ground: The Impulsive Ground (Shallow-Hearted)
    a. Endures for a little while then dies
    b. Impulsive heart: Tied to emotions
3. Thorny Ground: The Preoccupied and Unproductive (Half-Hearted)
    a. Thorns and weeds choke the life out; distracted and misfocused
    b. Preoccupied heart: Tied to self-image
4. Good Soil: Prepared-hearted, maintained, and productive
    a. Prepared heart: Tied to God and eternity

The parable of preeminence is designed to teach us kingdom dynamics and interactions, but make no mistake, the parable platforms the significance of the Word and the importance of the soil. If the seed is important, then the soil that it is being sown into must have value and worth as well. Every kingdom citizen must invest in soil maintenance and management because of the investment of the Word of God that is sown in our lives. We have this treasure in these earthen vessels!

Let's take a quick look at what God expects out of kingdom citizens or good soil citizens.

Characteristics of Good Ground

- Take God very serious
- Depend on God for the impossible
- Thank God for the possible

- Humble
- Spiritually aware
- Watchful of the enemy
- Value the Word of God more than life itself
- Attentive whenever the Word is being preached
- Take notes of the preaching or purchase CDs to really understand the preaching
- Have a library of preaching and teaching CDs that they refer back to every so often for spiritual empowerment
- Have daily or weekly devotions and readings in the Word
- Develop implementation strategies to incorporate the preaching into their daily lives
- Respect spiritual authority
- Esteem spiritual leaders
- Have an active prayer life
- Involved in the Great Commission
- Support the work of ministry with their talents, time, and treasure
- Celebrate God both in public worship and private devotion
- Expect and understand spiritual warfare
- Prioritize the kingdom of God
- Receive the care and protection of God
- Understand money and its primary purpose
- Have learned the secret of contentment
- Constantly growing in their relationship with God
- Understand times and seasons
- Have fellowship with other believers
- Guard their heart

The Results of Being Good Soil

- They yield or provide.
- They sprout or grow.
- They increase.
- They produce.

- They are not competitive with others or don't engage in comparable analysis.
- The Word works in their lives (Hebrews 4:12).
- They hear the Word.
- They accept the Bible as being the Word of God.
- They allow it to bear fruit.
- They maximize their potential thirty-, sixty-, and a hundred-fold; in Genesis 26:12, Isaac received a hundred-fold blessing.

Chapter Ten
The Bird

REMEMBER, THE PRIMARY CHARACTERS in the parable of preeminence are the sower, the seed, and the soil. However, like award-winning movies or plays, the parable becomes more interesting when characters have to face an adversary. In Christ's parable, the adversary is portrayed by the character of the bird. Farmers always have to contend with the loss of crop production caused by birds, which eat the seeds on the ground. Because of the vastness of the field, the sower cannot guard each seed from being eaten by the bird. However, birds are less likely to consume seeds that land on tilled soil. The parable teaches us that the bird comes immediately (Mark 4:15) and takes the Word that was sown in the wayside ground heart.

The bird, in our parable, represents Satan, the adversary to all who desire to live productive kingdom lives. Satan's [<sat-an-as'>, (Σατανᾶς)] name, before he fell from heaven, was Lucifer, which means "Daystar" or "Morning Star." *Satanas*, in the Greek language, means "adversary or accuser." The kingdom of God is in opposition with the kingdom of this world, which is ruled by Satan. In fact, he is called "the god of this world" in 2 Corinthians 4:4. The fourth gospel states that Satan is "the ruler of this world" (John 12:31, 14:30). Satan's present rule on Earth is made known in the temptation scene of Christ, where the devil declares that he has authority over "all the kingdoms of the world" (Luke 4:5–6).

As our adversary, Satan tries to disrupt the interaction between the sower, the seed, and you—the soil. He does this by attacking the relationship between the pastor and you and you and the Word. He knows if He can separate us from either the Word or our pastor, we will never produce. Satan, or the bird, always comes for the Word! Thus, if you are receiving the Word, the devil is not coming to attack you; he is coming to devour the Word! If you have no Word, you may be experiencing some challenges in life with everything from relationships to finances and everything else, but you are <u>not</u> being attacked by the devil—there is no reason for him to attack! If you have no Word, Satan is not coming for you.

It is critical to keep in mind that no matter where we are in life, we must continually contend with the attacks of the enemy. There is going to be a conflict. The reason many Christians backslide (or are re-inhabited) is because they are not prepared for this conflict. They live life as if serving Christ exempts them from the fight. However, we must remember that the devil is a military strategist who is strategizing on how to bring Christians back to him or how to detach them from the Word.

The parable of preeminence gives us insight into those attacks. In the parable, the bird attacks the soil for no reason other than to eat the seed. The Bible states that he comes to kill, steal, and destroy (John 10:10). Analogously, Satan's attacks on you and me are for no other reason than to remove God's Word from us. This is because he knows that the Word of God is the key to releasing our potential.

Many people believe that parental nurture or genetic predisposition are key determinates of our potential for success. They argue that people have a greater chance for success if they are mentored by successful parents or have an inherited ability to learn or lead.

However, this is by no means true. The Bible teaches that with Christ, we can do all things because He strengthens us (Philippians 4:13). Indeed, the promises of God are "Yes" and "Amen" to the glory of God (2 Corinthians 1:20)! Our nature cannot stop the purpose of God; Jesus destroyed the bondage of the cross. Those who are in Christ Jesus have been regenerated (or born again). Thus, the Apostle Peter admonishes us to partake in Christ's divine nature and to be born again, not of perishing seed but of seed that is imperishable, which is the living and abiding Word (1 Peter 1:4, 23). Knowing that our potential lies in the Word of God, the enemy will do everything he can to steal the Word from us.

When we were born, we were born into Satan's kingdom as citizens of darkness; Satan had dominion over us the moment we entered the earthly realm (Romans 6:14). We were so dominated by Satan that we did not even have the ability to discern truth from error. Before Christ, all men were born under Satan's bondage without an option. After Christ's coming, all men are still born under Satan's bondage, but we now have the option to choose another kingdom. It is Christ who breaks the dominion of Satan over our lives by making room for us to be able to see clearly enough to choose a different kingdom! Upon our acceptance of Christ as the sovereign in our lives, the enemy's possession of our lives was stopped. Jesus is the light of the world, and it is only when He was in our proximity that we were able to get a glimpse of His light—in the midst of our darkness—to see and choose Him.

When we were unsaved, we were not involved in warfare; instead, we were simply dominated by the enemy. But when we gave our lives to Christ, we entered into kingdom conflict. Matthew 12:43–45 states, "*When an unclean spirit goes out of a man, he goes through dry places, seeking rest, and finds none. Then he says, 'I will return to my house from which I came.' And when he comes, he finds it empty, swept, and put in order. Then he goes and takes with him seven other spirits more wicked than himself, and they enter and dwell there; and the last state of that man is worse than the first. So shall it also be with this wicked generation."*

Notice that the unclean spirit claims you as his possession when he says, "I will go back to *my* house." Satan wants to get back in, and he will do so if we let him. We often explain this scripture to new believers while overlooking its relevance to all believers. Our enemy, the devil, is not made of flesh and blood, but he is a spirit. As a spirit, he never gets tired, so he continuously and consistently returns to "his" house—you! We have to remember that, at all times, there is a demonic attack being launched against us, seeking to re-inhabit us; this attack will prevail if we are wayside, stony, or thorny ground when the Word is sown.

The presence of the Word is why believers will always experience spiritual conflict. The Bible states that Satan is the god of this world, and Jesus refers to him as the ruler of the kingdoms of the earth. The Bible teaches us that believers face hierarchical governments of evil spirits that control territories called principalities. Since the kingdom of this world is clashing with the kingdom of God, kingdom citizens are at war whether or not we desire to be. The enemy's plan is to stop you from fulfilling the will of God, by stealing the Word of God from your life. How is the Word of God stolen from the life of the believer? The Word of God is stolen from us when we no longer believe it. The Word of God is not effective in our lives unless it is mixed with faith (Hebrews 4:2). And true faith is made evident by actions; thus, we cannot just hear the . must also do the Word (James 1:22, 2:26). When we receive *rhema*, Satan designs attacks that are designed to make us doubt the Word we have received.

What often causes us to doubt the Word are our non-biblical belief systems, circumstances, and fiery darts of the enemy. These often cause us to doubt, making the Word of God of no effect in our lives. Doubt is natural, and some would say expected, when walking with God, whose glory and majesty are made known only through impossible situations. A writer wrote, "When God is about to do something great, He starts with a difficulty. When He is about to do something truly magnificent, He starts with an impossibility."[34] Difficult situations as designed to produce faith, and truly walking with God requires faith in Him and Him only. Jesus said to the man in the crowd whose son was possessed by a spirit, "'If you can believe, all things are possible to him who believes.' Immediately the father cried out and said with tears, 'Lord, I believe; help my unbelief!'" (Mark 9:23–24).

However, when this happens, we must utilize the tools God has given us for every doubtful situation:

- We must cast down every argument that exalts itself against the knowledge of God (2 Corinthians 10:5).
- We must not look at the things that are seen, for they are only temporary, but have faith (2 Corinthians 4:18, Hebrews 12:2).
- We must bind and loose in Jesus' name (Matthew 16:19).

Jesus said, *"Have faith in God"* (Mark 11:22). The promise of God is that if we believe and do not doubt, believing that we have already received them, when we pray, we will receive what we have asked.

The Bird and the Seed

When the sower sows the Word, we're supposed to expect the attack of the enemy. It is nothing unusual to be under attack. Understanding the kingdom means knowing that the enemy is always in opposition to you—"the kingdom of heaven suffers violence" (Matthew 11:12). The enemy is using every means necessary to stop the expansion of God's kingdom. Thus, as kingdom men and

---

[34] Armin Gesswein, Beliefnet's Inspirational Quotes, Retrieved from http://www.beliefnet.com/quotes/christian/a/armin-gesswein/when-god-is-about-to-do-something-great-he-starts.aspx.

women, we have positioned ourselves to experience the enemy's attacks. Many people don't understand that they are living amid conflict; however, kingdom citizens must know that. The kingdom of God is diametrically opposed to the kingdom of this world. By virtue of being a believer, we are at war, whether we choose to be or not. In order to enter God's kingdom, we denounce our former allegiance to the ruler of the kingdom of this world and declare belief, trust, and submission to the Lord Jesus Christ. The enemy claimed us when we were born, but once we renounced his kingdom, he began a lifelong journey to get us back (Matthew 12:43–45). The enemy won't stop until he steals our joy, destroys our families, destroys our health, and kills our spiritual lives. He does this by stealing the Word of God. For instance, have you said statements like these?

- Things would be better for me if my husband/wife would act right.
- Things would be so much better if I had a husband/wife who…
- Things would be so much better if my finances were in order.
- Things would be so much better if my business would come together.
- Things would be so much better if my children would just obey.

Statements like those above show that Satan has stolen the Word from us. The Bible states that our conflict does not derive from the people in our lives but from principalities, rulers of the darkness of this world, and spiritual wickedness in heavenly places assigned to our lives (Ephesians 6:12). To believe contrary is not to believe the Word of God, which means that it was stolen from you. It is our responsibility to protect and guard the Word of God sown into us. Our pastors cannot make us believe the Word when trials come to test our faith. His job is to sow the Word. In faith, we must know that God has given us all that we need to combat the attack of the adversary—He has given us *rhema*, the Word of God.

What put Satan out was the Word of God. The Bible says that believers are born again, not of corruptible seed but by the incorruptible Word of God (1 Peter 1:23). We became a new creation in Christ through the Word of God, seeded by a sower. That is how we received our new birth. But the Word is also what sustains the salvation received by our new birth. It is that which nourishes us, keeps us fortified, and protects us; spiritual growth comes through the Word (1 Peter 2:2).

The Bible teaches us that "if we walk in the light, as He is in the light, we have fellowship one with another, and the blood of Jesus Christ His Son cleanses us from all sin" (1 John 1:7). As we walk in the light of the Word, the Word is what illuminates things that we did not previously see. Because it allows us to objectively discern whether we are doing the right thing or the wrong thing, walking in the light provides us with the ability to change for the better. This change makes us more effective for the kingdom.

Satan understands that our effectiveness and success in life come from the Word. Therefore, he desires to separate us from the Word. He knows that if he can get us to replace the Word with "Christian" music, social activities, and community events, he will gain the victory in his quest to re-inhabit us. The Bible says, *"Finally, my brethren, be strong in the Lord and in the power of His might…that you may be able to stand against the wiles of the devil"* (Ephesians 6:10–11). This scripture lets us know that the devil will methodically come against us and that we will need God to withstand him.

The Bird and the Sower

While Satan attacks the Word of God in your life, he also attacks your relationship with the sower. Because he knows that we are no match for him without the Word of God, he attempts to create discord between us and sowers (pastors) so that we no longer receive the Word. He does this by causing us to examine the sower's life instead of believing in His seed. Many people refuse to receive the Word of God because of their perceptions of preachers. The truth is that our sowers are like many of us; they are undergoing the sanctification process too. However, unlike us, Christ has sovereignly chosen them to sow the Word of God. Thus, the issue is not whether they live perfect lives, because no human being can make that claim (1 John 1:8). The most important issue is this: Is your sower sowing the seed of the Word of God that is able to transform your life?

God promised to provide us with sowers that have a heart for Him (Jeremiah 3:15). Since it's difficult to receive a pure seed without a pure heart, we should assess the sower's heart for God by the effectiveness of the seed that they sow. Does God consistently speak to you (or give you *rhema*) when he preaches? Are you growing spiritually in tangible, biblical ways? If so, then he is your sower! When you have a sower who is sent by God, you receive a good seed. But with the Word comes the bird—you should expect attacks. You should expect Satan to highlight your sower's weakness in his efforts to instigate distrust in the sower and thus block you from receiving seed.

The combination of a sower, seed, and good soil produces a crop or fruit. Once the Word is sown, it matures and grows us spiritually so that we are effective disciples for our Lord Jesus Christ. The reference to fruit in this passage is the Newer Testament revelation of the passage in Genesis 1:28—be fruitful and multiply.

> *And He Himself gave some to be apostles, some prophets, some evangelists, and some pastors and teachers, for the equipping of the saints for the work of ministry, for the edifying of the body of Christ, till we all come to the unity of the faith and of the knowledge of the Son of God, to a*

perfect man, to the measure of the stature of the fullness of Christ; that we should no longer be children, tossed to and fro and carried about with every wind of doctrine, by the trickery of men, in the cunning craftiness of deceitful plotting, but, speaking the truth in love, may grow up in all things into Him who is the head—Christ— from whom the whole body, joined and knit together by what every joint supplies, according to the effective working by which every part does its share, causes growth of the body for the edifying of itself in love.[35]

When we mature in the faith, we become productive, and then we are able to receive and live the abundant life Jesus desires for us in direct opposition to the desires of Satan: "The thief does not come except to steal, and to kill, and to destroy. I have come that they may have life, and that they may have it more abundantly" (John 10:10).

---

[35] Ephesians 4:12–16 (NKJV).

Chapter Eleven
Kingdom Interactions

T HE PARABLE OF PREEMINENCE, in my strong opinion, is the gateway to practically understanding life as a kingdom citizen. As discussed earlier, we are in what I refer to as the Dispensation of Exaltation or the Kingdom Dispensation, a time when we are hearing, for the first time in centuries, an influx of teachings, music, and emphasis on the topic of the kingdom of God. Unfortunately, the topic of the kingdom of God is more than just a buzzword or catchphrase; it is a living experience with steep consequences and benefits. God has given this generation the ability to know the mystery of the kingdom in order to increase our understanding of spiritual warfare and to advance the kingdom message (Matthew 24:14). Hopefully, you have a greater understanding of the four dynamics of the kingdom: the sower, the seed, the soils, and Satan. In this chapter, let's explore how these four dynamics function in relationship with each other. Understanding how the four dynamics of the kingdom function and interact with each other will allow you to be a more effective kingdom citizen and better equipped to fight the enemy. How the dynamics relate to one another is germane to you having the mastery over Satan and not him over you.

There are four key relationships that a believer should understand when it comes to interactions in the kingdom. The Mark 4 parable teaches us about these relationships:

The Sower and the Seed – The sower is the one who sows the Word, and the seed is the Word of God. Thus, there must be a relationship between the sower and the seed. A sower is not a kingdom sower if he does not have a relationship with the seed. A kingdom sower exists to sow seed. Because he takes his spiritual responsibility of sowing seed seriously, he is not going to go to his supplier and just get any old kind of seed. He is going to inspect the seed to make sure it is good, check it carefully for quality, and then sow it. In addition, the sower must study and properly understand the seed. You should not be sitting in a ministry under someone who tells you they are sowing into your life but they have no relationship with the seed (meaning they have not engaged in any formal or structured program of theological study of the Word). The sower must understand the Word of God in its original context and has to be able to rightly divide the word of truth (2 Timothy 2:15). A sower must have sower skills and resources to interpret biblical passages. A sower does not sow what he wants to sow; a sower sows the Word in context! If they are sowing anything other than the Word, they are not sowing a kingdom message.

There is a very well-known female evangelist who preaches all over the world and who was interviewed on the *Larry King Live* show. Larry King asked her why she was a Christian and not a Muslim, Hindu, or Buddhist. Her response: "Because Jesus reached me first." *What???* I thought, *What if your spouse, when asked why he married you, replied, "Because you asked me first?"* Wrong answer! You want to know that there was no need for anyone else to ask, because they had experienced the best they ever had and there was no need to look any further. However, this is the type of response that is inevitable when a sower has no relationship with the seed. If this evangelist has no relationship with the seed, what is she teaching? The sower of the Word must have an intimate relationship with the Word; they are the experts in the kingdom about the will and Word of God.

The Seed and the Soil – The seed is the Word of God, and the soil is you (the condition of your heart when you hear the Word). The seed is sown into the soil. The soil takes the seed and allows it to grow and produce in it what would not have otherwise been produced. The seed needs the soil, and the soil needs the seed. The seed cannot become productive without the soil, and the soil cannot produce without the productivity of the seed. Hence, there is a symbiotic relationship that exists between the seed and the soil.

There must be a strong relationship between the seed and the soil. The soil is the condition of the human heart. If there is no relationship between a person (the soil) and the Word (the seed), this explains why this person may not hold a sower accountable to having a relationship with the seed. You only care about your sower's relationship with the seed if you have a relationship with the seed. Otherwise, it's really not that important to you. Because you are soil, you MUST have seed! If you find yourself not needing seed, seed getting on your nerves, or seed being too much of a distraction from the things that really matter in your life, you do not understand your position with God! When you understand that you are soil, you understand that without the seed, you cannot be productive or progress in the things of God's kingdom.

The Sower and Soil – The soil is the kingdom citizen, the sower is the fivefold ministry gift, and the seed is the Word of God. The sower has an intimate relationship with the seed, and the soil has a strong dependency upon the seed. These dynamics are kingdom dynamics and relationships. When the soil recognizes how valuable and dependent it is upon the seed, the soil attempts to get the seed by any means necessary. When the sower understands how crucial the seed is in the productivity of the soil, the sower ensures that the seed is quality because the life of the soil is dependent upon it. When the soil realizes how important the seed is to its own productivity, it creates value for the one who is responsible for sowing the seed. Satan understands how important these relationships/dynamics are, thus he desires to destroy or hinder the flow of functional and healthy relationships between the dynamics.

Your sower is your teacher (the one who sows the Word), and you are the soil. Because your sower has your seed and Satan is coming for your seed, you need two things from your sower: for him to sow seed into your soil AND for him to help till and guard your soil. Also, if you care about real productivity, you will demand that your sower has a relationship with the seed. Just imagine, if your sower has no relationship with the seed, what relationship would your sower have with you? A foul one!

In the contemporary church, many sowers are feeling underappreciated, undervalued, and burned out. Statistics suggest that in America alone, 1,500 pastors leave the pulpit a month, never to return. This is an attack of the enemy because the preacher is he that has been chosen and selected to sow seed upon the soil or feed the kingdom citizen with the Word of God. The relationship between a shepherd and the sheep is priceless. The Bible provides us with many models and examples of the shepherd–sheep relationship. The shepherd is called to feed the sheep, which makes the shepherd a sower. The shepherd is also called to protect the sheep as well as encourage the sheep. The shepherd's three greatest spiritual gifts for the sheep are the feed (seed), the rod (that which beats back the enemy), and the staff (that which catches the sheep when it falls). The shepherd is the greatest asset and friend to the sheep. The role of the shepherd is the highest role in the life of the sheep.

The Bible states that it is the shepherd that has the rule over the sheep (1 Thessalonians 5:12) and because of this, the shepherd or the sower should be highly esteemed (1 Thessalonians 5:13). The shepherd/sower is so important in the life of the sheep/soil that the Bible instructs the sheep/soil to obey and submit to the shepherd/ sower because they watch for your life and ensure the path to the eternal kingdom (Hebrews 13:17). The scripture states that this is a relationship that the soil does not what to sour or go bad, because it impacts the health of the soil negatively and causes the seed not to be productive.

The Seed and Satan – The seed is the Word of God, and Satan is the enemy who tries to steal it from the soil immediately after it is sown. Satan understands that if you (the soil) get the seed, you will become powerful! This is why he must disrupt the relationship of the sower and the soil and the seed and the soil if he is to have victory in your life. If he lets you get into the Word, start studying the Scriptures, and embrace God's Word, you will become something in the Spirit that you are not in the natural—a formidable foe to his kingdom. The enemy comes for the Word's sake. He does not want God, but he just doesn't want YOU to have Him.

In order to stop you from becoming what God wants you to be in the Spirit, Satan has to take the Word. Whether you realize it or not, you are nothing without the Word. The Bible says that the only ones who produce thirty-, sixty-, and a hundred-fold are those who were considered good soil. Kingdom productivity and progression are not found in lineage, education, affiliations, or associations; kingdom productivity comes only by the Word of God. You may think you are successful because you are bright, hardworking, and well-bred, but in the kingdom of God, you are who you are only by the grace of God!

What If I Don't Study the Word but I'm Still Under Attack? What's Happening?

I'll repeat this fact again because for so long, we have misunderstood the intentions of the devil. Kingdom citizens must understand what Jesus is plainly teaching: In the kingdom, Satan comes for the seed (the Word). If you are not studying scripture and you feel like you are under attack, you are simply self-destructing! Satan does not go after people. Satan does not go after possessions. Satan goes after one thing: the seed. Thus, if you are going through and feel under attack but you are not living according to the Word of God, it is because you are "tripping" or destructing all on your own—not because Satan is attacking you. The devil is not in your family or your finances; you are just making terrible decisions for your life. In fact, the devil is your partner; you are his friend and ally when you do not study the Word. You have absolutely nothing that Satan wants if you don't have the Word. Mark 4 clearly teaches us that it's not personal—it's the Word. It's not that Satan has anything against you as a person; he just wants to steal the Word from your life!

When Satan attacks you, according to Christ's teaching in this kingdom parable, he does so because of the Word. If the Word has the right to reign in you and you protect the Word by ensuring that you are good soil, the Word is going to produce a powerful and effective prayer life. If your prayer life is not present, it is not because Satan is fighting your prayer life; it is because he has taken the Word. There are a lot of people who pray, but they do not have the Word. Jesus says that we should ask the Father what we will in His name and He will do it. "In My name" suggests His will, His Word. How can you know the will of God without knowing the Word of God? You cannot have an effective prayer life without knowing God's will for your life.

The kingdom essentially is about the reign and rule of God, and this rule is also experienced by Satan and his kingdom. While we as believers are in spiritual battle, the battle is already won; John says that the greater one is in us (1 John 4:4), Paul says we are more than conquerors (Romans 8:37), and in the book of Revelation, it states that we overcame the enemy (Revelation 12:11). The believer understands that in the kingdom, his or her authority is in the written degree of the King: "as it is written." The power and authority we have over Satan is rooted in the authority of the King. The kingdom is the dominion of the King, the King's domain: His authority, rule, and reign. Dominion is a kingdom term. God as

King has dominion over Satan, sin, sickness and disease, situations, and the saints. God alone has dominion.

Yet there is teaching out there that states you are little gods and that you have dominion; you are to rule the earth and take back the devil's territory. In scholarship, we call it "dominion theology." This interpretation of theology is not well respected at all among those in scholarship, because it has no theological basis. This theology ultimately suggests that the believer will rule the world; however, the Bible doesn't teach that. In fact, apocalyptic literature suggests the opposite. Humankind once had dominion in the Garden of Eden. Because they did not rely on God, but on "the knowledge of good and evil," they lost that dominion in the fall, and Satan became the god of this world (2 Corinthians 4:4). However, at the cross, Christ defeated Satan, and through the resurrection, He regained dominion as fully man in the person of the Son of Man. Thus, the scripture does not teach that you and I have dominion over Satan; Christ has dominion, but in Christ and through the Word of God, we have authority over Satan! However, since humankind was created in the image of God, there are shadows of godliness and morality that exist in us but always remain vulnerable to Satan's devices.

In 1 John 5:19, it states, "We know that we are of God, and the whole world lies under the sway of the wicked one." When we study the New Testament, it is very clear that the two kingdoms are in great conflict and that there is no such place as neutral. If you are not for God, you are by default against Him. Satan's minions, the demons, still afflict humankind. Paul understood that the world was subjugated to Satan or evil powers (1 Corinthians 2:8, 15:24–27; 2 Corinthians 4:4). When people cannot see that they are standing for the kingdom of Satan, it is because Satan has blinded their minds. Satan literally controls the minds of unsaved people who do not know Christ—they are under the power of the evil one. How does Satan exercise this power over them and control the world?

By the lust of the flesh, lust of the eyes, and the pride of life (1 John 2:16). Luke writes that the kingdom vision is to turn people from the dominion of Satan unto God (Acts 26:18). That is the ultimate definition of our productivity and that for which Satan attacks the saints. But our God reigns forever and ever! Ephesians 1:21 states that Christ is far above all principalities and might, dominion, and every name that is named, not only in this age but in the age to come. Christ regained dominion through the cross and the crown and now sits on the throne ruling and reign in the life of kingdom citizens upon the earth.

- 1 Timothy 6:16 states about Christ, "*who alone has immortality, dwelling in unapproachable light, whom no man has seen or can see, to whom be honor and everlasting power.*"
- 1 Peter 4:11 says, "*...to whom belong the glory and the dominion forever and ever.*"
- 1 Peter 5:11 states, "*To Him be the glory and the dominion forever and ever.*"
- Jude 25: "*To God our savior, who alone is wise, be glory and majesty, dominion and power, both now and forever.*"
- Revelation 1:6: "*and has made us kings and priests to His God and Father, to Him be glory and dominion forever and ever.*"
- Revelation 5:13b: "*Blessing and honor and glory and power be to Him who sits on the throne, and to the Lamb, forever and ever!*"

This is the gospel of the kingdom—that the King took the reins back and is now ruling and reigning among those who repent and call Him Lord and enter the kingdom! Welcome to the kingdom!

Kingdom Books by Dr. Dana Carson

If you are a person who is serious about walking with the King and fulfilling the King's preordained purpose you were birthed for, Dr. Dana Carson has penned the following works as a labor of love to assist you in your transformation. In order to fully understand the Kingdom to the point where you can explain it and teach it to others, these books are "must reads."

One True King: Surrendering Our Attitudes at the Altar of Revival
ISBN: 0-9780615387-9-5

The Christian church is facing its finest and final hour: a REVIVAL of unprecedented effectiveness! God is placing the church back into Kingdom alignment so that we may experience power and authority such as the contemporary world has never seen. Before we can experience this revival, we must tear down the idols that prevent us from seeking first the Kingdom of God. This book will assist believers in making the Kingdom of God a reality in their lives and move them into the next dispensation of theological awareness. It is time for the people of God to become His own special people – a people who honor and serve the One True King!

The Doors of the Church Are Closed
ISBN: 0-97816047794-7-9

The Doors of the Church are Closed is one of the most relevant 21ˢᵗ century writings to the church. Statistics suggest nearly 4,000 churches are closing with only 1,200 to 1,800 opening annually. Fewer than 20% of Americans attend church and 97% of churches didn't win one convert last year! The church has exchanged its mission of Kingdom expansion for popularity and wealth. This book identifies the root causes of the contemporary church's failures and raises some monumental challenges to believers. This book is a must-read for the Body of Christ and for those who desire to fulfill the will of God in their lives.

Lord Help! I'm Trapped in the Church!
ISBN: 0-9746616-4-3

This book is extremely insightful! Dr. Carson has captured the reality of many contemporary Christians who detect something is wrong with the Christian church, primarily based on their own feelings of hunger and unfulfillment. By teaching what the church should be doing, Christians will finally be able to 'put their finger' on what the church is missing – Jesus!

In this book, Dr. Carson describes how many of the traditions of the church have caused people to put their faith in unfounded teachings, Through the principles you will be able to accurately asses their relationship with God and His church. This book provides biblical tools that will empower Kingdom citizens to resist the devil and experience high levels of Kingdom satisfaction and effectiveness. Dr. Carson has done it again by shining a light and providing ways that will help those who are attempting to transition from spiritual mediocrity to spiritual significance. This is a must read for anyone who desires to experience greater levels of God's presence in this life, regain their Kingdom focus, and ensure their place around the throne!

The Kingdom, the Church, and YOU! Issues That Impact the Lives of Every Believer
ISBN: 0-9746616-7-8

This book will revolutionize your thoughts concerning the Kingdom of God and its relationship to the church and how they mutually impact your walk with Jesus Christ. The issues discussed in this book are very seldom discussed in church settings, but greatly impact your walk with Christ and with other believers. Dr. Carson, Dr. Young, and Dr. Grizzle provide insight on the Kingdom of God as scholars who are committed to the practical presentation and understanding of the Kingdom concerning modern cultural and theological issues. Your understanding of the Kingdom, the church and YOU, will never be the same again!

Introducing the Kingdom: Your Basic Guide to Understanding the Kingdom of God
ISBN: 0-9746616-8-6

The phrase, "Kingdom of God," has become a powerless catch phrase in many churches today.
Few believers really understand what the Kingdom of God is or how to practically live as a Kingdom citizen. They have been trapped in the church and church traditions. Now, a generation is rising up, seeking to sincerely understand this Kingdom! Introducing the Kingdom was written to answer the questions any true seeker will have. It gives you the basic ideology and practices of Kingdom citizens. With this book, you will learn what it means for God to be the one true King of your life. You will never wonder again whether you are seeking first the Kingdom of God and His righteousness – you will know!

Kingdom Change and Transformation: Embracing a New Future
ISBN: 0-97707389-4-6

Research suggests that change is a very difficult process, and as a result, very few individuals ever change! Unfortunately, life and its design are structured for constant change; everything and everyone is in a constant state of flux, changing either for the best or for the worst. Dr. Carson explains, from a biblical and clinical perspective:

- Why change is needed
- How to practically employ change initiatives
- How to position yourself for greater levels of success

This book will teach you how to achieve the much needed and wanted change that you have earnestly pursued, possibly for years, but have been unable to achieve. This book will revolutionize your thought process as you learn how to think different and become a different Kingdom you!

Let's Get Real! How Total Transparency Can Transform Your Total Life
ISBN: 0-97707389-4-6

In this book you will learn how to be real with God, yourself and others. You will find the keys to removing the mask of doubt and fear which hide the person you were born to be.

On these pages you'll find:

- Why you must unlock the secrets of your heart
- How God views the mistakes of your past
- The necessity of being honest with yourself

- What the Word says about self-esteem
- The keys to personal liberation
- How to become free from guilt and shame
- and much more!

Incarnational Leadership
ISBN: 0-9746616-5-1

Winston Churchill. Napoleon Bonaparte. Martin Luther King, Jr. Lee Iacocca. What do each of these men have in common? On any Google search, these distinguished gentlemen are listed as some of the greatest leaders of all time. Their leadership accomplishments are unparalleled, their exploits unmatched by few, if any, of their peers within their respective generations. Thousands of books have been written about their uncanny abilities to effectuate change in their contexts through their leadership. Further, with technology facilitating the immediate translation of these writings into hundreds of languages, people around the world on every continent study their carefully penned leadership strategies closely, attempting to walk in the footprints of these legends and replicate their successes. However, despite all of the books on the shelf and all of the best efforts to replicate the successes of these leadership legends by would-be leaders worldwide, the vast majority inevitably fall short. How could this be? Why do so many fail when following the blueprint of what should yield inevitable success? Perhaps the answer is in the model.

Sound Doctrine: The Fundamentals of Biblical Faith
ISBN: 0-9746616-2-7

The Bible states that men will not endure sound doctrine and that there will be a great apostasy or falling away. Theological researchers reveal that we are living in a biblically illiterate context in the Age of Information. Paul's prophetic words to Timothy are coming to pass - men love themselves more than God...even in the church. "If you love me, keep my commandments", most people who attend church or call themselves Christian cannot explain or defend their faith. In this work, Dr. Carson plunges through fundamental biblical concepts and tenets and make them easy to understand for everyday believers. He examines some of the most fundamental doctrines of the Christian faith from a Kingdom perspective. The book addresses such topics as: angels, heaven and hell, the Holy Spirit, salvation, spiritual warfare, and much more! The Bible states that the end times will be a highly deceptive time, and the only way to navigate through the traps of deception, designed by the enemy to shipwreck your faith is to continue in doctrine. Undoubtedly, this book will empower and strengthen you to endure to the end!

Kingdom Marriage: Trouble in the Flesh
ISBN: 13-978-0-615-38789-5

Take a fresh and mature look into the marital relationship through the writings of Dr. Dana Carson. With sound biblical and relational teachings designed to assist couples, Dr. Carson shares four keys necessary to a healthy, Kingdom relationship – keys that will assist the husband in becoming a more  godly, effective, and fulfilled leader of his home and keys that will assist the wife in becoming all God designed her to be, utilizing her influence to encourage and build her marriage! This book is not only a "must read" for every married couple; it is also for singles who desire to marry one day.

Kingdom Discussions in Theology: Exploring the Basic Tenets of Theology
ISBN: 978-0-9859244-5-4

In the age of, what some would refer to as, biblical illiteracy, there are very few church leaders who are committing themselves to understanding theology proper. The book, *Kingdom Discussions in Theology* is written to provide Kingdom leaders with a broad base of discussions in theology from a Kingdom perspective. The church did not begin in North America or during European colonization, and Dr. Dana Carson probes the annals of theology from a historically accurate perspective. Dr. Carson takes a look at biblical themes that every Kingdom leader should understand as they mount the stage of leadership responsibility. This book addresses topics such as God, the Trinity, Soteriology, the Reformation Period/ Roman Catholicism, Pentecostalism, Evangelicalism, and many more topics. This book will empower the reader to have a greater grasp of some of the most major themes of the Bible. This book connects contemporary readers with the historical beliefs of the church – beliefs that have defined her for the last 21 centuries. Please join Dr. Carson for *Kingdom Discussions in Theology*.

The Apostles' Doctrine: The Foundation of Biblical Faith
ISBN: 978-0-9859244-4-7

The book *Apostles' Doctrine* focuses upon the fundamental doctrine of the Kingdom of God. This book is designed to provide the reader with a sound basis for their belief in Christ and His gift of salvation. The book of Acts suggests that the early church followed the apostles' doctrine (Acts 2:42). Apostle, Dr. Dana Carson has written this book to expound on the seven foundational tenets of the faith, recorded in Hebrews 6, from a Kingdom perspective. Luke opines that these basic Kingdom principles must be learned and mastered in order to achieve spiritual maturity. Everyone who is serious about studying the scriptures, and desires to become strong in the faith and not able to be tossed to and fro by every wind of doctrine, must read the Apostles' Doctrine. The scriptures declare that, in the last days, men will not endure sound doctrine (2 Timothy 4:3). However, the Bible states that you and I MUST pay attention to ourselves and to the doctrine. If we do this, we will save ourselves and those who hear us (1 Timothy 4:16). It is imperative to know doctrine if you desire to "endure to the end" in this Laodicean culture, and not be defeated by the devil because of ignorance.

The Apostles' Doctrine is your key to a lasting Kingdom relationship with God!

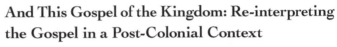

And This Gospel of the Kingdom: Re-interpreting the Gospel in a Post-Colonial Context
ISBN: 0-9746616-3-5

And This Gospel of the Kingdom is another brilliant work from the pen and spirit of Dr. Carson. In this book, he revisits the traditional view of the gospel of the Kingdom of God and concludes that we have proclaimed the gospel with a misaligned emphasis placed upon the death, burial, and resurrection of Christ. He thoroughly proves, from the Holy Scriptures through the dispensations of time, that Christ came preaching the gospel of the Kingdom, not the gospel of the resurrection. Dr. Carson opines that the message of the cross and the resurrection was never intended to be the end goal, but the means to the end – the Kingdom! This book:

- Explains how the gospel has been misinterpreted and that the authentic gospel of the Kingdom calls men to subject themselves to the rule and reign of God through Christ Jesus.
- Reveals that God desires and it is His will to become Lord, not just Savior, of the believer's life – the new dominating force in life that fills the void left by Satan's dominion.

This is a must read for every serious believer and church leader! It will surely cause you to re-evaluate your belief in the work of Christ as the Passover Lamb and re-evaluate your commitment to Jesus the Messiah!

The Kingdom Man & The Kingdom Woman: How to Fulfill God's Purpose for your Life! ISBN: 978-1-9402640-1-1

Have you ever wondered what a Kingdom man and a Kingdom woman looks like? In this book, Dr. Dana Carson once again provides a Kingdom decoder to help us to understand the biblical roles of men and women. In his own unique way, Dr. Carson explains genders in the Kingdom that will astound and amaze you! This book illuminates the Jewish background of biblical passages that speak to gender distinction and differences. Then it gives practical insights that will assist Kingdom men and women in fulfilling God's Kingdom purpose for their lives. After reading this book, you will understand what inspired church men and church women to embrace the Kingdom and the Kingdom mandate for men and women, and you will never again be confused about your Kingdom

The Crown & the Cross: Understanding the Kingdom of God
ISBN: 978-1-9402643-8-7

The Crown and the Cross will revolutionize the way you define your faith as Dr. Carson challenges you to rethink your interpretation of scripture, based upon a Kingdom perspective. This revolutionary look at Jesus Christ highlights His crown and not merely His cross. This book will open the minds of those who have been trapped in traditional views of the church that have caused stagnation and disinterest. We invite you to explore a fresh look at the cross of Christ through the lens of the crown of Christ and become empowered to live a victorious life in the Kingdom! Your walk with God will never be the same!

Printed in the United States
By Bookmasters